MEDIATION BEYOND COVID

HACKS, CRAICS AND CROCODILE TEARS

Compiled by

SARAH M BLAKE

Copyright © Sarah Blake

First published in Australia in 2023
by KMD Books
Waikiki, WA 6169

All rights reserved. No part of this book may be used or reproduced by any means, graphic, electronic, or mechanical, including photocopying, recording, taping or by any information storage retrieval system without the written permission of the copyright owner except in the case of brief quotations embodied in critical articles and reviews.

Because of the dynamic nature of the Internet, any web addresses or links contained in this book may have changed since publication and may no longer be vaild. The views expressed in this work are solely those of the author and do not necessarily reflect the views of the publisher and the publisher hereby disclaims any responsibility for them.

Cover design & layout: Dylan Ingram
Doodle images: Ming Johanson

A catalogue record for this work is available from the National Library of Australia

National Library of Australia Catalogue-in-Publication data:

Mediation Beyond Covid/Sarah Blake

ISBN:
978-0-6456765-7-0
(Paperback)

CONTENTS

SARAH BLAKE
SETTING THE SCENE — 1

KENNETH CLOKE
FORWORD — HOW COVID BEGAN AS A CONFLICT, BECAME A CRISIS AND CAN BE BLOCKED FROM BECOMING ANOTHER ONE — 7

CHRIS MUIR-SMITH
CRUNCHY CONVERSATIONS MATTER — 19

CLAIRE HOLLAND
MEDIATING BEYOND BORDERS A GLOBAL COMMUNITY — 35

HAYDEN WILSON
CREATING OUR PROFESSIONAL COMMUNITY — 49

HAYLEY JARICK
A MORE SUSTAINABLE FUTURE — 61

HAZEL HERRINGTON
WE RISE TOGETHER — 81

JOANNE MCMULLAN
DEVELOPING CHANGE RESILIENCE — 93

LAURENCE BOULLE
DISLOCATING TIME REIMAGINING SPACE — 109

MEGAN MACNEILL ACCELERATED LEARNING	123
MIKAL SANZ PEÑA CHOOSE YOUR OWN ADVENTURE	143
MING JOHANSON TIME TO THINK	157
PAUL SILLS THE GLOBAL TOUCH	173
ROAR THUN WAEGGER NEGOTIATING WITH THE BRAIN IN MIND	191
SAM HARDY BOUNCING FORWARD NOT BACK	207
SHANTI ABRAHAM MATHEW POLLINATING OUR MEDIATION LANDSCAPE	221
SREE SWAMINATHAN ADAPTABILITY IS THE KEY TO SUCCESS	235
SUSAN ANDREWS ALLOWING THE FLOW	249
VIKRAM SINGH BRINGING PEOPLE UNDER THE TREE	263
TRENT PETHERICK ASSESSING COST DIFFERENTLY	281
SARAH BLAKE CONCLUSION — PULLING IT TOGETHER	295

SARAH BLAKE
SETTING THE SCENE

Navigating conflict is hard. It often takes up too much time and money, it reduces innovation and productivity and impacts relationships and reputations. So, we avoid it.

We avoid it because it seems too hard, too messy, too confronting. These are the stories we tell ourselves about conflict, and they justify our avoidance. But they aren't the only stories we tell. On the flip side, perhaps your stories are that every conflict is an opportunity to fight, to gain more control, more influence and more power. Whatever your own conflict story is, it's highly likely your deep belief is that conflict is 'bad' and therefore it's easier to react to the pain than to lean into the opportunity.

I can remember the exact moment when I found the confidence to lean into conflict.

It was messy and painful, I likely had tears running down my face as I contemplated what was being thrown at me. It was unfair, people who were older, more experienced and should have known better were treating me with complete disrespect, I knew it wasn't really about me – but it still bloody hurt. It was confusing, and I was filled with insecurity. In this moment of deep desolation, I opened my heart and found my anchor. I found a deep connection inside me – a capacity to just be in the moment and know, really know, that despite how confusing, confrontational or challenging the conflict, I could survive. This deep inner strength has rooted, found its footing in the soil of this land, in my family and the knowledge of the business of dispute resolution that I have crafted, nurtured and discovered since. It is not an easy path; conflict will never be a comfortable thing for anyone, but knowing my foundations, knowing when to hold the line and when to give, has helped forge me into something stronger.

I have never been more grateful for this knowing, this knowledge and these skills than during the recent pandemic.

In late 2019, COVID emerged, bringing with it a whole new set of problems, conflicts and confusion that we all had to deal with. Humanity faced a rapidly changing environment, high levels of uncertainty and the hard reality of death. We saw natural wonders, when people could see the stars for the first time in cities, and painful division when families, neighbours and communities clashed over issues of vaccinations, lockdowns and more.

None of us were immune from the pressures, from the pain and yes, conflict. As a first responder, my husband spent significant time away from our family. I had to juggle being a mum, teacher, businesswoman (and occasional wife) all at the same time. Here in Western Australia, we had a very different experience compared to other states and nations. Many of us felt both grateful and guilty, but almost all of us knew someone who died, someone who suffered or lost relationships, their business, job or income. Like most people, my own relationships were tested, my kids didn't like me being teacher and my business was booming. It was my mediator skills that helped me keep moving forward. Sometimes only one step a day, but keep moving I did.

For leaders across disciplines, this time has required a different sort of response; they have had to develop the capacity to rise above the crisis and provide safe ways forward. Conflict didn't go away, it changed, and in many instances, grew, with differences dividing workplaces, communities and families. We ended up in positional debates of 'right and wrong' where nuance and the middle ground were silenced. We are still feeling, and dealing with, that impact.

In 2020, a small group of mediators gathered on Zoom to share stories as they struggled to adapt, adjust and survive whilst supporting people through conflict. Over a glass of gin, laughter and sometimes tears, we learnt a lot. What really stood out was our capacity to just be there for each other, and this was powerful. It created a deep sense of connection, an inner circle of support. We would meet fortnightly initially, and as things returned to 'normal', we met less and less. Instead of making time for each other, we got busy and back to work, and I found myself missing this connection. But it also made me realise how grateful I was for the space to talk deeply and honestly, not just about how we deal with conflict, but how we deal with the messiness of life.

It got me thinking that others too might benefit from these stories, these fireside chats. Perhaps if we could make conflict less 'bad' then people and especially leaders might be more able to lean into those hard conversations with curiosity. What I hope is that you, as the reader, might see yourself in some of these stories, that you might breathe for a moment and say, 'It wasn't just me.'

The last few years have tested us all. Our resilience 'buckets' are running low, and it's unlikely that pressures will lessen, they will just change. As leaders, be it in industry, commercial, community or the dispute resolution field, we are all being called to step up and into this messy business of humanity. People are struggling to know what to do with these hard conversations, to these different and difficult BIG issues. People are tired of the fight and perhaps are ready for problem-solving. But they need help to do this, they need us to create safe spaces for dialogue and so they need us to show them how!

This collection brings together professionals across disciplines who are experts in dealing with conflict, confusion and change. From mediators, lawyers, HR, marketing and executives, they are sharing their insights to help you better manage the complexities of negotiation, conflict and problem-solving.

I hope these real-life stories of gritty leadership and hard conversations, spiced with a touch of humour, will make it easier for you to talk about conflict. I wanted to find a practical way to help you navigate this space with clarity, confidence, and yes, some fun. Conflict will always be a part of our lives, but it doesn't have to drive us. We need to balance that out with lightness, moments of connection and joy.

I have gathered these authors together because I know they are all, in their own ways, shaping change in their spheres of influence. They are stiving to make a difference, not just a profit. Their stories are from the heart, but they are also deeply practical. Over the past few years, we have had to weather storm after storm, and this book hopes to make it just that little bit easier for you to move forward.

So, pour yourself a gin (or a cuppa) and be prepared to discover that hard conversations don't have to result in a fight. With a little preparation, some key skills and a growth mindset, peace is possible.

KENNETH CLOKE
FOREWORD
HOW COVID BEGAN AS A CONFLICT, BECAME A CRISIS AND CAN BE BLOCKED FROM BECOMING ANOTHER ONE

So let us honour the dead and dying, the heroes in hospital gowns and grocery aprons. Let us commit that their sacrifices shall not have been in vain and dedicate ourselves to turning these otherwise marginalised and sidelined insights in the direction of global problem-solving.

'The political class … is strategically incapable of addressing even short-term crises, let alone a vast existential predicament. Those who govern the nation and shape public discourse cannot be trusted with the preservation of life on Earth. There is no benign authority preserving us from harm. No-one is coming to save us. None of us can justifiably avoid the call to come together to save ourselves.'

GEORGE MONBIOT

'Adventure is a crisis that one accepts, crisis is an adventure that one refuses. And it is possible at every moment in our life, to decide whether the rupture that comes upon us is here to destroy us or to make us evolve, to force us to find in ourselves resources that we didn't know could exist.'

BERTRAND PICCARD

Lives have been lost, so let's be clear, not mince words, or politely ignore what COVID has done, and the way our chronic, unresolved social, economic and political conflicts got in the way of saving them. On the most obvious level, the wealthiest and most powerful individuals, communities, races and countries lost fewer lives than those less advantaged.

What was worse, hostile, conflicted, hyper-polarised political groups – especially in the US and other wealthy countries – turned a simple health issue into a fight for political gain, promoting anti-Chinese and anti-Asian prejudices, conspiracy theories, unscientific remedies, foolhardy risk-taking, withholding lifesaving vaccines and equipment from others, putting pharmaceutical profits before human life and similar follies. Why? And more importantly, what can conflict resolution teach us about how to avoid similar outcomes in the future? That is the goal of this book.

THE LARGER PROBLEM

The problem, unfortunately, extends far beyond COVID. We appear to have entered an era of escalating conflicts and crises; one in which our survival as a civilisation and as a species increasingly depend not on military prowess, economic might or political dominance, but rather on our ability to listen empathetically, communicate nonviolently, solve problems jointly, negotiate collaboratively, decide consensually, act collectively and resolve conflicts mediatively.

They therefore also depend on our capacity to appreciate diversity and dissent, to engage in dialogue with those who think differently, to build trust between former foes and to bridge and *dismantle* the social, economic, political, cultural and environmental barriers we have erected over centuries to distance ourselves from – rather than resolve – our conflicts with others.

Chief among these barriers is the *form* of our political discourse and the hostile character of our governments and nation states, which were historically created to defend hierarchical, win-lose social, economic and political systems that are *grounded* in domination, privilege and prejudice; that rank public health, social improvement, environmental sustainability and human life – even our *survival* as a species – as less important than national pride, private wealth, corporate profitability, destructive growth and competitive advantage over others.

As a result, we are facing intensifying conflicts and crises around the world that pit the popular demand for solutions to a growing number of escalating problems, including health care, against the competitive institutions, wealthy elites, corporate giants and political bureaucracies that have created, exacerbated, ignored, tolerated, covered up and profited from them.

What is worse, the nation state *itself*, perhaps the most powerful problem-solving mechanism ever created by human beings, has become an obstacle to finding solutions, partly because the problems and crises we increasingly confront exceed its bounds and are now global in scope. Sovereignty, prejudice, factions and nationalism more and more stand in the way of transnational communication, global cooperation and social consensus. As a result, politicians find it nearly impossible to address the general, global, species-interests of all – *except* selfishly, competitively, adversarially and in ways that defeat or diminish their capacity for global collaboration.

Yet global cooperation by means of the nation state is *essential* in trying to solve these problems. Without some form of international problem-solving that is *vastly* stronger than individual nation states or the United Nations is presently able to muster. Without the widespread adoption of a broad range of transnational collaborative, consensus-building and conflict resolution methodologies, global problems will increasingly go unsolved, conflicts will fester, divisions will deepen, crises will arise and these will, at some point, if unresolved, connect, creating larger, universal, fundamental, *general* crises and new pandemics, leading to catastrophes that could threaten our survival.

To avoid these lower order outcomes, we require higher order skills. What are these skills? They include, at their core, the ability to listen and empathise with those who are different; to work together to solve common problems; to engage in dialogue over disagreements; to build consensus; to negotiate collaboratively;

to mediate conflicts; and to seek restorative justice in unifying and empowering solutions.

In these ways, it becomes possible not only to face the conflicts and crises created by the global pandemic, as well as those aggravated by prejudice, polarisation, insurrection, climate change, environmental devastation and similar problems, but to minimise their destructive effects, evolve to higher forms of social, economic and political relationships, and hopefully, at some point, stop slaughtering, hating and trying to dominate and control one another.

WHAT WE CAN LEARN FROM THE PANDEMIC

What happened during the pandemic? Suddenly, in a moment, everything shifted. Unimaginable outcomes were revealed as mere habits, assumptions, patterns of thought, feeling and behaviour, driven by an unquestioning desire for comfort and security and a fear of what we do not know. These then limited, channelled and recycled our perceptions, leading us to see as solid what was actually liquid or gaseous.

What matters now, after health and survival, are vision and values and a willingness to think deeply and creatively about what we witnessed and experienced – not only the suffering and loss of life, but the singing, dancing and celebration of life, the courage and deep desire for connection, the importance of love and collaboration that took place everywhere, every day, in the midst of all this loss.

On the one hand, we were, and are, deeply divided from one another by this virus – nationally, racially, economically, culturally, religiously, politically, even individually – through fear and social distancing. On the other hand, we were, and are, united by it, as all humanity now faces the same problems and must learn and practice higher order collaboration and conflict resolution skills in order to survive them.

The logic of division is fear and hatred of others, of narrow nationalism and egotism that regard other people as threats to our survival. The logic of unity is love and caring for one another, of globalism and altruism that experience others as essential to our own survival – not just physically, but mentally, emotionally and spiritually, socially, economically and politically. These different responses lead to fundamentally different outcomes.

Just imagine what would happen if all the doctors and nurses, farmers and grocery workers, scientists and firemen had decided to stop working and just look out for themselves – and the result is the same for every problem, and on a smaller scale, for each of us.

Fortunately, most of us were not required to interact personally at close range with those who have been infected with the virus, so our courage and dedication needed to take a different form. We need, for example, to resist xenophobic efforts to label this the 'Chinese virus'; to offer our services as mediators, facilitators and conflict coaches to first responders; to agree to work online at no or reduced fee with couples, families and organisations in nations and communities that have been locked down or are in crisis; to keep alive the idea that social distancing does not have to mean social isolation, and can be counterbalanced by song and story, and everyday celebrations of empathy and heroism.

We can even *thank* the virus, for reminding us what is precious; for forcing us to realise that without the courage of health care workers and grocery clerks we personally might not have survived; for asking us to have the courage not to abandon each other, not to put joy and happiness on life support, not to lose sight of the higher order visions and values we are now being asked to live by.

These are the visions and values of *species* solidarity, of global cooperation and coordination, of sharing and supporting one another, of valuing our differences and abandoning *no-one*. They are the visions and values of dialogue and collaboration, mediation and negotiation, forgiveness and restorative justice, empathy and mindfulness, love and kindness.

So let us honour the dead and dying, the heroes in hospital gowns and grocery aprons. Let us commit that their sacrifices shall not have been in vain and dedicate ourselves to turning these otherwise marginalised and sidelined insights in the direction of *global* problem-solving. In the end, it doesn't matter whose end of the boat is sinking – with pandemics, as with global warming and environmental degradation, we sink or swim together.

We have learned from the pandemic that we are all facing death, and are therefore one, connected by crisis and undivided by conflict. And we have also learned that we are facing it differently, and are therefore many, separated by race, gender, nationality, age, religion, wealth, occupation, social class, political beliefs, emotional vulnerability, and physical well-being, and divided by conflict.

What we have *not* learned sufficiently or everywhere is how to turn our differences into deeper and more powerful expressions of empathy and compassion; how to strengthen I/thou communications and relationships with our opponents; how to use the pandemic to repair the cracks in our systems; and how to evolve to higher *orders* of conflict that reveal and require higher orders of resolution.

We have learned that we can withdraw from the world and

still be in it. We have learned to be socially and emotionally connected while physically distant. We have learned the importance of science and the equal importance of art, music and dance. We have learned that we can be courageous, even when we are frightened. We have learned the meaning of touch, contact, intimacy and connection; of having time to reflect, exercise and meditate; of the centrality of celebration and loss. We have learned the depth, extent and intricacy of our interdependency. We have learned the value of slowness, and that when we stop even for a moment, our skies clear of pollution, global warming slows its pace, whales and dolphins return to our shores and we are able to take pleasure in the beauty of nature and each other.

We have learned that global problems cannot be solved using national or local methods; that death and loss touch all of us; that political conflicts can be deadly; and that it doesn't matter whose end of the boat is sinking. We have learned that it is easier to face death together, even if each of us dies alone, and that looking out for ourselves requires us to look out for each other.

What we have not *yet* learned is how to hold on to these lessons and not return to an addictive cycle that leads only to future crises and conflicts; how to love one another enduringly, and that in all the conflicts we experience between 'us' and 'them', there simply *is* no them, there is only us. We have not, in short, learned the most fundamental lesson in all of conflict resolution: that *every one* of our conflicts contains opportunities for learning, discovery of self and other, and evolution to higher, better and more satisfying relationships. And that the pandemic is pointing our attention toward precisely those outcomes.

Doing so will require us to bring conflict resolution *directly* into the social, economic and political arena. It will require us to strengthen global collaboration through dialogue, negotiation and mediation; to invent interest-based forms of political discourse, economic activity and social problem-solving; and to find new ways of assuaging the pathological belief in medical conspiracy, suicidal resistance to common sense health measures, hostility to science and art, and fear and rage toward migrants and minorities that are also infecting us.

None of this will be easy or quick. But, as mediators, we have been too silent, confused, reactive and avoidant in applying our skills and knowledge of conflict resolution to the chronic social, economic and political conflicts that are impacting our response to COVID, and to other, equally pressing issues, and have been so for far too long, and are paying the price.

So let us honour those who have died and those who are still dying, the heroes in hospital gowns and grocery aprons, the friends and families who have suffered – and let us commit that their sacrifices shall not have been in vain by dedicating ourselves, our energies and intentions, our knowledge and skills, to keeping these lessons alive until we have transformed them into renewed hope for a better world, and return – not to our old, conflicted lives – but to newer, more collaborative ones, enriched by learning and dedicated to preventing the next pandemic from being so costly – so we do not just come back to life, but come back better. Read, and consider how you might contribute to doing so.

Kenneth Cloke
Santa Monica, California

BIO

Ken Cloke is a world-recognised mediator, dialogue facilitator, conflict resolution systems designer, teacher, trainer, author and public speaker. He has been a pioneer and leader in the field of mediation and conflict resolution for the last thirty-seven years. He is co-founder of Mediators Beyond Borders, based in Washington DC. The organisation supports individuals, organizations, communities and governments around the world in building conflict resolution capacity and conflict literacy, focusing on under-served communities.

He has done international work in conflict resolution in over twenty-five countries, including Armenia, Australia, Austria, Brazil, Canada, China, Cuba, Denmark, England, Georgia, India, Ireland, Japan, Latin America, Mexico, Netherlands, New Zealand, Nicaragua, Pakistan, Puerto Rico, Scotland, Thailand, Ukraine, the former USSR, United Kingdom and Zimbabwe.

kencloke.com
linkedin.com/in/ken-cloke-4b66433/

CHRIS MUIR-SMITH
CRUNCHY CONVERSATIONS MATTER

Maintain the line. Good processes keep people safe and maintain legal compliance. It's not meant to be tough, it's just a safe way of operating.

Negotiations during COVID included one client wanting to conduct their work from a tree.

TELL US ABOUT WHAT YOU DO AND WHAT YOU LOVE ABOUT WHAT YOU DO.

I'm a Human Resources professional, with over 30 years of experience working within the fields of Human Resources, Industrial Relations, and Dispute Resolution. My career has included roles such as Human Resources Consultant and/or Manager (in-house or corporate), Trade Union Official and independent Human Resources Consultant in the public and private sectors within both New Zealand and Australia. Throughout my career, I have often found myself required to engage in dispute resolution processes, which could be a simple deed of settlement, to a complex mediation process required to settle a Collective Bargaining Agreement, and/or an Enterprise Bargaining Agreement.

Four years ago, I launched a bespoke Human Resources Consultancy based in Western Australia with my husband. Our current client base is an eclectic mix of small to medium-sized businesses, often working within a cross-section of industries and states across Australia. One of the most common questions I am asked as a Human Resources professional is *"What is Human Resources?"* This often leads to a conversation many employers and/or consultants believe is the *"dark side"* of my profession, commonly referred to as "Dispute Resolution." It is the dark side of Human Resources, which has led to referrals from employers and/or consultants, requiring support to attend Fair Work or Western Australian Industrial Relations conciliations, the management of a change process or in-house mediation between parties.

As a Human Resources professional, I get a great deal of satisfaction in supporting my clients' transition from a state of conflict, by either agreeing to a resolution, and/or a process to achieve a mutually agreed resolution. I also take great care to educate and empower my clients throughout this process, in general, an employer doesn't decide, *'I'm going to deliberately operate outside the guidelines of best practice or legation,'* instead, they make decisions at the time they believe is the best fit, based on their situation. Or they are given flawed advice from consultants who are not qualified, indemnified, or frankly, do not have the practical experience to support a business requiring Human Resources, Industrial Relations, or Dispute Resolution expertise.

TELL US A LITTLE ABOUT HOW COVID IMPACTED WHAT YOU DO AND HOW YOU ADAPTED?

I don't believe we have come out of COVID – it's still in play. Okay, we may not be under mandates that require vaccination or be in a situation where employees are required to isolate or wear masks, but all employers are required to ensure they provide a safe workplace for their employees, which means all of our clients need to future-proof their businesses for another event similar to COVID.

As a Human Resources professional, my objective throughout COVID was primarily to empower our clients to navigate the often inflexible and rigid framework of Federal and/or State (Western Australia) employment legislation and to build on their employment relationship with their team or individual employees. It needs to be noted that employment law, has historically been amended to support the political ideology of a government of the time, without any consideration taken into the potential impact of an international event such as a pandemic. For example, in the early months of COVID, the Fair Work Commission was required to provide, a greater level of flexibility to the Fair

Work Act 2009, in the short term, to ensure small-to-medium employers were able to operate while meeting their obligation as an employer.

However, a number of our clients attempted to continue to operate with absolutely no understanding of how COVID restrictions would have an impact on their employees and their positions as "Business Owners and/or Company Directors." In some instances, we had clients who were mortified to find their employees did not like them, and when their team were asked to accept a greater level of flexibility with their terms and conditions of employment (such as a request to take leave), their employees often refused. For many, this was a tough lesson to learn, with one of our clients losing their business because their primary objective was to maintain a healthy cash flow, regardless of the impact on their workforce.

COVID also provided many individuals with a platform to express themselves in a dysfunctional manner that ordinarily would not have been accepted in the community or their workplace. However, other individual team members were absolute gems. They were, as one of our clients described, *"the light in the darkness."* Amid the conflict, they were the calm rational colleagues and leaders who said, 'Hey it's okay, we will get through this. Don't panic and let's all treat each with respect".

Dispute resolution in this climate required a greater level of reliance and empathy, often working with an employer or employee to acknowledge that COVID was the trigger for conflict, not their colleagues, employer or employee's ideology and/or their reaction to the pandemic, along with lockdowns and mandates for example.

TELL ABOUT DEALING WITH CONFUSION, CHANGE AND CONFLICT SINCE WE'HAVE BEEN IMPACTED BY COVID

As I have previously mentioned, I believe social media, and the Internet in general, played a dangerously destructive role in many individuals' lives. For many, they were sucked down a virtual rabbit hole, very much influenced by information that was not based on medical facts and/or data. There were some right-wing groups, I believe, who had no other purpose than to cause distress. And if you were an employer or employee that did not understand the purpose of these communications, which was to cause misery and confusion, you could find yourself virtually in the dark, uncertain of what and whom to believe.

For example, when various states rolled out COVID mandates across Australia, my team were required to have crunchy (challenging) conversations with employees to advise each individual of their rights in the workplace and their obligation to adhere to various COVID mandates if they wanted to keep their role. It was a very difficult time for the employee in question. These situations most commonly required every resource I had in my conflict resolution and mediation toolbox, and or practical experience, to find a resolution.

I believe it doesn't matter what the issue you are about to mediate is, or the parties involved, the one thing you need to have, is absolute transparency and clarity around the process. Even though we had emotional situations with clients and their employees, there were many instances where we had to be tough. It was not meant to be offensive, but we had a process we needed to follow, and you cannot just say to someone, '*here's the process*' and then not explain why. Many times, my team spent a huge amount of time educating our clients, and then educating their employees, because they needed to understand how and why the process was being rolled out.

Employees needed to understand their rights and their ability to influence the process. Sometimes their capacity to influence the process was marginal and they believed they were being disadvantaged. However, my team needed to take the time to explain what the implications would be if they chose to make certain decisions, for example, to be vaccinated or not. Even though it was a personal choice, we had to make them aware that if they chose to, 'these are the options available.' If they chose not to be vaccinated, we had to make it clear what it would mean to them. Even though many people felt they had no choice, this was not true, and this is something I want to be clear on; people did have a choice. However, maybe when things fell apart, when it came to decisions, say, to be vaccinated or not be vaccinated, or an employee did not do their research, social media played a significant impact on many people's decision-making process.

One of our clients had a large number of employees, in multiple locations in various states, who believed they should be treated differently (from other employees) because of the nature of their industry, and how adhering to a COVID mandate could potentially have a negative impact on the community. The employees in question felt they were entitled to be treated differently from other workplaces. However, when they were informed that they would be required to adhere to the COVID, mandate in their state, some of their reactions were intense and incredibly challenging. This ultimately led to several leaders in the workplace resigning from their roles because they did not have the managerial experience or they found themselves in circumstances, which required an advanced level of resilience to have the "crunchy" but productive conversations. And that is a fair call, after all, it was an international pandemic, and I do not think there was anyone who could say they had lived through anything like this before. Every day was a new day and a new challenge, and sometimes we just needed to roll with it.

This is why it was so important to have clarity around the process. Whether an employer and/or employee, believe it or not, having a clear process keeps all parties safe. If everyone understands what the process is there for, and how their choice is going to impact the process, as well as what resources may be available to them if they choose to make a decision, then that is an amazing thing to have in place. Not everyone likes to have a process because it means it may take them to the end of the road where they do not want to be. But frankly in situations such as conflict resolution and COVID, you cannot just wing it.

Throughout COVID, I had several conversations with less experienced professionals in my field who said, 'Oh, no… we just need to be nice; we need to be empowering and we need to be flexible,' and often what happened in those situations, was that they found themselves completely overwhelmed. Many times, as a result of this approach I had to intervene, sit them down, and take my colleagues back to stage one. I had to explain it to them from a legal premise, what the requirements were, the milestones that needed to be met, along with the reason.

Quite often, employers also found themselves in a legal forum because they wanted to be flexible. They wanted to be empathetic and empower their employees, however, in doing so they unwittingly did not adhere to COVID mandates and/or employment law. This is what I mean by needing to have a process in place to keep all individuals safe, but also to be legally compliant. It is not meant to be tough; it is just a safe way of operating.

From a conflict perspective, a fair process requires all parties to work in good faith with each other, but it does not mean all parties will agree on the process or even the outcome. Therefore, transparency and accountability are an absolute must, regardless of the process. For example, within the Human Resources and Employment Relations arena, you always need to achieve an end game. Unfortunately, some professionals tried to manipulate the process (end game), to obtain personal gain from COVID. They used the pandemic as "a cash cow," finding opportunities to charge excessive rates as opposed to ensuring their clients made it to the other side of the pandemic.

These were the occasions I frankly had to use a huge amount of self-control and professionalism to stay on task. We [my team] always held the line and were always respectful in the manner in which we worked through these situations.

TELL US ABOUT THE CRAICS, CROCODILE TEARS AND STANDOUT MOMENTS FROM THE LAST FEW YEARS

At the time, it was not so funny, but in hindsight, I can now laugh about the situation:

I had one client in particular who, once again found they had a significant number of employees who had been influenced by social media; in this case, they had been influenced by a platform promoted by lawyers with a right-wing mentality, and they were offering legal services at significantly reduced rates. One employee in question, decided, as part of the consultation process to determine his alternative work arrangement, "such as asking an employee to perform different duties or to work from home." He had concluded that the Wi-Fi from his workplace (office), extended beyond the carpark to a nearby tree.

As part of the consultation process to determine an alternative work arrangement all employers were required to consider, an employee's request for an alternative work arrangement, which required a meeting to discuss potential options. In this case, the employee brought his lawyer with him to a meeting via Zoom, where he wanted to negotiate how and when he could work from the tree and speak to his clients (sitting at the bottom of the tree in a camp chair) via his mobile phone, which he intended to disinfect upon the completion of each meeting with his clients.

So, as you can envisage, this led to some very interesting conversations, with the employee's lawyer, where I have to admit I did lose my patience, asking if his advocate had obtained his law degree from the back of a Weetbix packet! Not my proudest moment, but I was dumbfounded as to how a reasonable and responsible member of the legal profession would attempt to advocate for such an illogical alternate working arrangement. We did find a resolution in this matter, however. It took my team a considerable amount of time to take the employee and his lawyer through the process, in detail, to find an acceptable resolution.

In another case, the employee in question (a tutor) did not want to work from a tree, but her car, which she wanted to park just outside of her workplace. To provide context, at the start of COVID, medical clinics and centres were requiring patients to refrain from entering their reception areas. In many cases, clinical staff were requesting patients to stay in their cars until they had accessed the potential for cross-infection.

The tutor (who worked for a very small client, three employees) decided she did not want to come into the workplace at all. She kept referring to the fact that her local GP was happy to have people sitting in the car park, and she wanted to tutor her class sitting in her car on a mobile phone or put the class on speakerphone. Once again, as in the previous example, a car cannot be determined as an alternative work arrangement to the workplace. It was a similar dynamic, the employee was genuinely terrified about coming into the workplace. She kept referring to her local doctor who was not happy for unwell people to come into his waiting rooms. She could not understand why she would be asked to come into the workplace and work with a large number of children, whom she believed, were going to make her unwell. A slightly different dynamic, (without an advocate supporting the employee) but once again, her decision-making process was based on fear, due to misconceived notions about COVID.

I believe fear has dominated rational thinking for many employers and employees. Even now, I think if we were able to go back and support some of those individuals, there would be a very different discussion. At the time there was a considerable amount of pressure put on people, which lead to high levels of anxiety and stress. People were genuinely terrified. I think for a large number of the employers and employees in question if they were required to make the decision not to be vaccinated, again, they would be very much aware they might not have an income, while they still had a mortgage or rent to pay, still had to buy food, and still had to look after their family.

There were also legitimate cases where an employee was unable to be vaccinated because of serious health conditions, which led to very robust discussions with our clients explaining that some employees had legitimate exemptions. They were legally compliant and could not be kept from the workplace. There were discussions with employers and their teams, on how they could not exclude employees with a legal exemption. There were instances we had to discipline employees because they did not want to be around people who were not vaccinated. This often resulted in a polarised community. In some cases, the employer did not want their employees with health exemptions to be in the workplace, which required our team to educate our clients, unpacking in detail how an employer could not remove an employee's basic terms and conditions of employment.

Because of COVID, I have found the frequency of having "crunchy" conversations increasing. It felt like we were having these conversations all day, every day, for at least eight months, while previously we would meet with a client maybe a couple of times a week. During COVID, it was just one, long, ongoing, crunchy conversation.

I am also convinced that some of our clients who are leaders and CEOs, whom we are still working with, are suffering from post-traumatic stress. Quite often they have been incredible leaders, but the personal toil COVID has had on those individuals has been significant, to the extent a number of these leaders who once loved what they've been doing for the last 10-20 years, just one day said, 'I can't do this anymore. I just don't want to be working. I don't want the responsibility.' This is a common discussion we've had with a lot of leaders in this space. They do not want the responsibility and they no longer want to deal with the same level of anxiety they've had to manage over the last 2 years.

SHARE YOUR HACKS, INNOVATIONS, OR LEARNINGS THAT HAVE EMERGED FROM THIS TIME

Moving forward, leaders need to significantly increase their level of resilience. I believe a large number of applicants, are now going to think twice about applying for roles where the buck stops with them, especially if they are a leader or CEO in large organisations. Or even as a leader in an organisation, with only 20-plus employees. I have noticed within the recruitment side of our consultancy, how many incredible leaders and/or qualified, experienced managers, are applying for lesser roles; for example, we have found some leaders are applying for bookkeeping roles when they used to be Chief Financial Officers.

I believe emerging leaders, in any profession, need to have a greater sense of self-worth, and resilience. They need to be forgiven – by themselves, their colleagues, and their employers. For myself, there were many days when I came home and would beat myself up because I was not able to achieve the outcomes I wanted for my clients. In those moments, even a Human Resources professional can be caught up in the heat of the moment, where I failed to acknowledge I needed to be more forgiving and kinder to myself.

Moving forward, I believe there needs to be an emergence of a new style of leadership, with a significant degree of emotional intelligence. It must be noted that this is not just about being empathetic or empowering your team without actually increasing productivity, and it is not just about how to hold the line while maintaining resilience. The mental fitness and resilience required by any leader in today's workplace will need an individual who can create boundaries while also understanding the people dynamic with some empathy and flexibility. It is the evolution of personal emotional intelligence, which I do not believe can be taught in any workshop. It is 'emotional intelligence plus.'

Leaders of tomorrow will need to be prepared to hold people accountable, while at the same time, having their team trust and respect them. They will need to be able to get the best from their team, whilst employees must be prepared to excel for them.

LOOKING FORWARD, WHAT DO YOU THINK MIGHT BE SOME LASTING TRENDS OR INFLUENCES

COVID has highlighted the need for strong and meaningful processes. Leaders will need to create a process that is succinct and makes sense;

one where you can clearly explain why an objective is going to be required and/or a legal obligation must be adhered to, for example.

Let us go back to emotional intelligence. Sometimes you may need to roll out a process that may not be pleasant, so it is imperative to have the ability to communicate 'why' the process has to happen, along with the resilience to ensure the boundaries are held strongly in place.

I have learnt that even though we have always had these tools in our toolbox, we have never had to rely on them quite so heavily as we have recently. We also have other things we can do to achieve an outcome, but I think moving forward, with the potential level of anxiety that may impact, not just the workplace, but the local community, you need to be COVID-ready and COVID-savvy. Employers will need to have policies, training, and business plans in place to take on board the possibility of COVID Mark II or III.

It will no longer be acceptable for a Business Owner or Director not to have an understanding of the following:

What are you going to do if it happens again?

How are you going to survive as a business?

What is your plan? (Remember 'just winging it' is no longer an option for any business.)

YOUR TIPS FOR DEALING WITH PEOPLE DYNAMICS DURING CONFUSION, CHANGE AND CONFLICT

- You have to find common ground by identifying elements the parties (employer and employee) have in common, you can accomplish;
- Assisting the parties to see each other's perspectives (and more likely to understand each other's arguments);

- Showing the parties how similar their goals are so they can move closer to a settlement that achieves both sides' goals; and
- Decreasing the parties' anger. It is harder to be angry with someone with whom you have something in common with;
- You've got to have structure.

All discussions and processes must have a structure. It is so important to have a clear and simple pathway to an outcome. However, do not restrict it to a specific timeframe, have some flexibility around the timing. As long as you have a paper trail from which you can provide reliable data, there is no reason why the parties cannot extend the timing, as rigid timelines can put all parties under extreme pressure.

If you back yourself or others into a corner and say, 'a decision is needed by noon today.' for example, the parties are not going to have a sensible conversation with you. Make space for good decision-making, and make sure it is well documented.

- Follow up with people

Always follow up. Do not just say, 'right, that's it we're done. It was nice working with you,' and then never get back to either party. All mediation requires a follow-up process to ensure no one is still aggrieved by the outcome. It may not be you directly who does the follow-up, but ensure you know that everyone has closure.

Remember, it could be five years down the track, and something could pop up when you least expect it and you are not prepared. Small issues left to fester become bigger issues.

BIO

Chris is a highly experienced HR professional with 30 years of expertise, 22 of which in senior roles spanning human resources, training, dispute resolution and industrial relations. She has worked with companies ranging from global firms to small businesses in roles across the business, banking, specialist HR, and not-for-profit sectors.

Chris believes that local support within our community plays an essential role in success; her own mantra is Live, Buy and Support Local. Chris is an active member of the Mandurah Districts Rotary Club while personally supporting several local charities. In 2021, Chris was awarded the 2021 Peel CCI Individual Excellence Award at the Alcoa Peel Business Excellence Awards, and in 2022 won the Micro Business of the Year Award at the 2022 RKCC Mineral Resources Regional Business Awards.

linkedin.com/company/hr-dept-rockingham-kwinana-and-peel
facebook.com/HRDeptRKP/

CLAIRE HOLLAND
MEDIATING BEYOND BORDERS
A GLOBAL COMMUNITY

Mediators can provide support to parties who are not able to effectively negotiate directly, and the impact of a well-supported conversation should not be understated.

In the legal system, you tend to pick one side, and then you come up with a story, narrative and evidence that supports that one side. Then you fight with the other side until there's a final outcome. It didn't sit well with my core values and my worldview at the time. That's when I discovered alternative dispute resolution and I knew this was what I wanted to do with my life.

TELL US ABOUT WHAT YOU DO AND WHAT YOU LOVE ABOUT WHAT YOU DO

I am the director of the Masters Program of Conflict Management and Resolution (CMR) at James Cook University (JCU). JCU runs a full postgraduate masters program focused on the skills, knowledge and personal attributes required for people who want to be conflict specialists. Graduates of our program develop the skills to be more competent at dealing with conflict and to be able to run processes to assist other people to more competently deal with conflict. What I love about the way in which we run the CMR program is that it's very skills based. It focuses on the micro skills people can learn one day and apply in their workplace the next day. I get to work with a diverse range of students because conflict is so multidisciplinary. We have people in the classroom who come from a wide variety of backgrounds, including defence, health care, policing, HR, education, hospitality and politics. Everyone's experience is varied, which makes the learning in the classroom so valuable as everyone shares their experiences of conflict in their own work contexts and the different ways they apply their newly acquired CMR skills and knowledge. It's such an amazing learning environment, and I get really excited and energised by being involved as a lecturer, facilitator, trainer and coach.

The lecturers in the CMR program are 'pracademics' because we're practitioners as well as academics. I'm also a practicing mediator, mediation trainer, conflict coach and group facilitator. I work in Queensland on a number of mediation panels, but also privately, so I can arrange ad hoc mediations and conflict training. I think it's important that people teaching CMR skills ground their teaching in practice.

In terms of my own journey to becoming a conflict specialist, I initially wanted to be an economist. I applied to do a combined economics and law degree as I thought the combination with a law degree would strengthen my résumé when I entered the job market. I discovered that I quite liked the law, but I also found it very adversarial. In the legal system, you tend to pick one side, and then you come up with a story, narrative and evidence that supports that one side. Then you fight with the other side until there's a final outcome. It didn't sit well with my core values and my world view at the time. That's when I discovered alternative dispute resolution and I knew this was what I wanted to do with my life. It was an amazing feeling to find a career path that aligned with my interests and skills. I love working with people to build their confidence in managing their own conflict and assisting in the development of habits that will positively impact future interactions.

My first job after completing my Masters of Mediation and Conflict Resolution was working on the Thailand-Myanmar border in refugee camps as a mediation specialist. In this role I worked with a team to support access to conflict resolution processes for camp residents – because if you've got a group of ten thousand people in a confined space, there are going to be everyday conflicts! I've also worked internationally in the Philippines as a capacity development officer, and as a group facilitator for Scope Global. I've since completed a Graduate Certificate of Education and I've nearly finished my PhD, focusing on positive psychology and legal education.

I'm currently deputy chair of Mediators Beyond Borders Oceania (MBBO). We set up the group during the pandemic in 2020, after attending a Mediators Beyond Borders International (MBBI) conference in Bali, 2019. It was a great experience being part of such a diverse group of mediators and conflict specialists, but many of us in the Oceania region felt challenged by time zones of the North American and European based groups. We've since established the MBBO group over the last couple of years, focusing on communities in Oceania.

TELL US A LITTLE ABOUT HOW COVID IMPACTED WHAT YOU DO AND HOW YOU ADAPTED

There are a number of specific examples that come to mind, primarily around communication. We created MBBO so we could participate with like-minded colleagues through engaging in thought leadership, developing ideas and opportunities for interactions between practitioners providing or involved in conflict support services across our region. However, with the literal lockdown of countries, COVID cut off many opportunities for people who were living in different locations to come together to have conversations.

When the pandemic first occurred, it meant a lot of the conversations initially ceased, and it was an interesting time to reflect on how communities of practice could continue to work together. In our work with MBBO, we were very aware of the challenges of even getting access to laptops for some of the communities we were talking with. One particular example is a conference we virtually attended and MBBO had put together a panel on *Conflict Management, Environment and Sustainability*. A colleague called in from China, and at that time, Shanghai was in strict lockdown. But they managed to phone in. On the day, a colleague from Fiji wasn't able to attend because Fiji had just gone into a localised lockdown, and our colleague didn't have internet at home and couldn't travel to the office. COVID impacted our connections across borders, quite significantly.

COVID was challenging for so many people, but for those without access to reliable internet and good phone reception, isolation had a new meaning!

I work on a number of mediation panels. Before COVID, I would do mediations for my local community in face-to-face meetings, but I also had experience doing phone mediations for other jurisdictions. The phone is quite interesting, because it's not online in the sense that you can pick up facial cues; you are purely relying on vocal cues. It can be a challenge for the parties and the mediator if one or both of the parties don't have access to good phone reception. In my own practice, I would be in the middle of phone mediations, and someone would say, 'I'm having trouble hearing. I'm on my farm, standing in the middle of a field, on a little bit of an incline, trying to get reception. I might cut out, but we'll just do the best we can.' It's amazing the challenges some people go through just to join a conversation. Being able to engage in conversations and have effective communication is so important. Mediators can provide support to parties who are not able to effectively negotiate directly, and the impact of a well-supported conversation should not be understated. COVID has highlighted the importance of being flexible in communication and the importance of having multiple communication channels available.

In terms of training, COVID certainly impacted our ability to deliver face-to-face training and that had a key impact for people who have different learning styles or learning preferences, like the kinaesthetic, visual and interpersonal learners. A number of students and professional development (PD) participants really struggled with the trend to move learning and PD online. For some the experience was great, but in the online environment, you don't necessarily get the same triggering of emotions, like anxiety and stress, that flood of cortisol when you're being asked to negotiate, mediate or manage a group. And that is key when developing personal skills. I do believe that for many people their skills and knowledge in the online delivery of services has increased, however I'm not sure if that directly translates to similar competencies in running face-to-face services. I'm also not sure the extent to which people who aren't comfortable learning online, may not have chosen to attended PD or higher education on the online learning platforms. I wonder if this will have a future impact on the number of people entering the field or choosing to specialise in mediation and conflict support services.

TELL US ABOUT DEALING WITH CONFUSION, CHANGE AND CONFLICT SINCE WE'VE BEEN IMPACTED BY COVID

We all have an internal 'whiteboard' in our minds. I like to use this as a metaphor for the mental load people carry with them. On the whiteboard, we put all the concerns and issues that are arising for us. And during COVID, there were a lot of issues. Things were changing quickly, and many circumstances felt like they were out of our control. Added to that, if you talk to someone in Australia right now, there are probably going to be additional issues for people who have been impacted by natural disasters. In Australia, we've experienced floods, fires and unusual weather activity. The flow-on effects, such as unstable living conditions, changes to employment, lack of tradespeople to rebuild homes and core infrastructure – anyone in small business is suffering. There are ongoing supply chain issues, which lead to delays in getting parts or materials to build. We have inflation and a rising cost of living. Parents are worried about the new school year and what to do if kids get sick. On a world scale, we have a war in Ukraine and world leaders behaving in unpredictable ways.

Some people are directly feeling the effects of those issues, for others it may be the feeling of emotional contagion. I think it's important to acknowledge many people are experiencing a heavy mental load, and there is a lot going on their whiteboards. Therefore, people are primed to be triggered at the moment. The culmination of local events, global events and COVID has also changed a lot of priorities for people. The behaviour people now exhibit could be quite different to how they would have behaved before COVID. There are different conflicts resulting from clashes of values, expectations and perceptions of acceptable behaviour. Some conflicts are simply the result of people trying to meet their core needs in these unprecedented, complex and challenging circumstances. Mediators can assist parties to gain greater awareness about what is going on around them and the choices they have available to them. The available choices may not be the parties' preferred options, but hopefully there are available options that everyone can live with. I think mediators can play an important role in supporting parties in conflict to recognise the extraordinary mental load they may be carrying and acknowledge how hard the current circumstances are for some people, as well as helping parties navigate their internal whiteboards during these periods of uncertainty.

TELL US ABOUT THE CRAICS, CROCODILE TEARS AND STANDOUT MOMENTS FROM THE LAST FEW YEARS

I do a lot of mediations on residential tenancy issues. This has been a particularly challenging context over the last few years. We're currently experiencing a housing crisis in regional Queensland.

Rent has gone up exponentially and the cost of living is also increasing. Some families have wage and income insecurity, but they feel they don't have a choice but to accept the higher rents and sign new leases. I'm increasingly seeing conflicts arise with delays in rental repairs due to the cost of materials or the supply chain issues and lack of labourers. In regional areas where there have been natural disasters, like the floods in particular, many of the tradespeople migrate to where the flood-affected areas are. That leaves a gap in the workforce in regional towns. Suddenly people are paying a high rent for a house that doesn't have a working stove for six to eight weeks. Tenants are not getting the value of what they're paying for, and landlords are often not agreeing to a reduced rent while waiting for repairs, as they know they could get another renter in without any delay.

Another standout story for me was a workplace mediation between two colleagues and a manager during COVID when people couldn't go into the office. Communication was primarily occurring online, via email and Facebook Messenger chats. For people who hadn't previously communicated this way, it led to a lot of miscommunication, often from perceived slights, due to different written communication styles and different personality types. It meant certain employees were often responding to online messages in anger. In this particular instance, the workplace conflict quickly escalated. It got to a point where employees were being subjected to long, inappropriate rants about other employees' capabilities and actions, being woken up at 2am by a message with pages and pages of very poorly communicated language that would never have been accepted in the office. If the triggering incidents had occurred in a face-to-face environment, I'm quite certain a lot of the written communication (sometimes just a stream-of-consciousness outburst) would never have been said out loud. In this workplace's online environment, there was no online culture for checking in about misunderstandings or perceived slights. As a result, the relationship between the two staff members had broken down to such an extent it was unsalvageable, and they could not continue to work together.

COVID has challenged the personal managerial styles of many leaders. Some managers have the mindset that you must be present at work and be 'seen to be working' in order for work to be done, while other managers say 'I trust you' and employees can feel empowered to get their work done through flexible and often innovative means. Work-from-home directives have also highlighted how different personalities operate in different environments. Some people can work productively in a low-stimulus environment, while others need high stimulus to be focused and energised. When there is a disconnect between employees' preferred working style and managers' mindset, I'm seeing conflicts arise around return-to-work agreements and work-from-home options.

I think there are a lot of issues that might have been latent or unconscious conflict before that are now being bought into the conscious arena. This is leading to an increase in change and decision-making fatigue because our brains are constantly trying to predict what's going on in our current complex environment. When individuals are constantly feeling like things are in chaos or out of their control, it can be exhausting gathering information to make informed choices about what to do next. Many of these decisions used to be made on autopilot, but we're now having to bring a lot of previously unconscious decision-making into a consciously considered and renegotiated arena. It's leading to ill health, fatigue and eventually burnout for some people. There's a lot of potential for conflict when people are operating in a state of fatigue and exhaustion. That being said, I've had meetings with people who have called up asking for assistance saying, 'Just want to let you know, I've been impacted by the floods. I'm now living in a tent while I have COVID. My workplace is requiring me to still go to work, because I'm a critical worker, while I'm taking care of family.' And ... and ... and ... The combination of events impacting individuals is beyond anything I would have heard before COVID. I have found it amazing how much people were dealing with and the fortitude of many individuals.

SHARE YOUR HACKS, INNOVATIONS OR LEARNINGS THAT HAVE EMERGED FROM THIS TIME

An important learning for me is around 'awareness of self'. Working during this time of chaos provided an opportunity for self-reflection and reflective practice. I was able to come to a realisation about what my core safety and security needs are. This was a useful learning because our basic needs will probably (hopefully) never be impacted in such a way as they have been during this global pandemic.

I think as a mediator, an important aspect of our role is also supporting other people to have that awareness of self. If your safety and security needs are extremely important to you and you feel they are being impacted, then the decisions you make in a time of chaos will be around risk avoidance. That could be very different to how you operate in a normal environment where you could be quite a risk-taker. The realisation that there is a difference in your environmental triggers an increased self-awareness of your decision-making influences and their effect on your behaviour can be a huge revelation to some individuals. Just knowing that information can support better communication and conflict management during difficult times.

LOOKING FORWARD, WHAT DO YOU THINK MIGHT BE SOME LASTING TRENDS OR INFLUENCES?

Linking to our conversation around latent conflict earlier, I believe COVID has bought a lot of underlying structural and inequality issues to the surface that maybe hadn't been considered priority issues before. I think more conversations have opened up as a result of COVID and hopefully there will be better engagement with these core issues moving forward. It will depend on the consistency of engagement by key parties. When you have communication channels that change over time, sometimes the frequency of interactions change and it can have an impact on either escalating or de-escalating a conflict and the emotions around it.

I see that the environmental conflict space is going to become increasingly important to talk about. Those conversations will include how people are involved in decisions that can impact their communities and the livelihoods of people around them. It's unlikely the conversations will ever lead to a resolution, but it's important to have continuous conversations as long term engagement plans for managing conflict. Through MBBO we are looking to open up more conversations, recognising that local wisdom is key when dealing with people in conflict. Sharing experiences and having conversations around 'how do you do things? And what works for you?' can help communities learn from how things are done in neighbouring countries.

YOUR TIPS FOR DEALING WITH PEOPLE DYNAMICS DURING CONFUSION, CHANGE AND CONFLICT

- Take a step back and really think about what is going on. In the JCU Masters Program we call this conflict analysis. 'What is going on?' is a very important first step, because there's always three questions: 1) what is going on for you? 2) what is going on for other people? and 3) what is going on around the conflict? Maybe the conflict is something you can choose not to engage in 'right now'. Or maybe the timing of engagement in the conflict could be changed with greater awareness of the ebbs and flows of what's going on around the conflict?

- Recognise there are always going to be some elements of conflict that cannot be resolved. My colleague, Dr Judith Rafferty, and I are focusing on research around this for ongoing conflict. How do we recognise conflict that is resistant to resolution and will persist over time? Having a plan for ongoing and enduring conflict will look quite different from a plan for conflict resolution.
- Self-care and awareness of self. You may be going through conflict yourself when you're trying to support other people in conflict. This can create ill health and burnout if you're putting yourself in a state of distress. In order to help others, it's important to fit your own oxygen mask first. Be reflective in your practice as a professional and debrief with other mediators and engage in activities to ensure you are feeling supported. With many conflict specialists, they do work individually and can start to feel isolated. Reach out to your networks when you need to and engage with your communities of practice.

BIO

Claire is a leading academic in the conflict management and resolution field in Australia. In addition to being a practicing mediator, conflict coach, workplace facilitator and trainer, Claire brings her knowledge of current scholarship and research into practice. As a result, she is at the forefront of developing best practice and thought leadership in this field. As the director of the Conflict Management and Resolution Program at James Cook University, Claire developed and leads the number-one postgraduate law program in Australia that has 100% student satisfaction rating over the last five years.

Claire is a founding board member and vice-chair of Mediators Beyond Borders Oceania (MBBO). The mission of MBBO is to develop regional capacity and skills for peace; promote conflict management and resolution skills and processes; and share techniques of mediated, non-adversarial, collaborative and dialogue-based conflict management and resolution in Oceania.

mbbo.com.au
linkedin.com/in/claire-holland-b1463160

HAYDEN WILSON
CREATING OUR PROFESSIONAL COMMUNITY

If you don't, as a mediator, create that environment and then create the conditions where people can have hope, well, then you're not going to be a mediator for very long.

Water cooler conversation.

TELL US ABOUT WHAT YOU DO AND WHAT YOU LOVE ABOUT WHAT YOU DO

I'm a commercial litigator and mediator based in Wellington, New Zealand. I've been mediating for eight years, alongside my litigation practice in one of New Zealand's largest legal firms. I first studied mediation as a way of being better for my clients in my litigation practice, but I was quickly drawn into the mediation world.

I love the variety of my mediation practice and the practicality of a strategic problem-solving focus. Most of all, though, I love the creativity and collaboration within the mediation community, something that came to the fore during COVID, when we all had to figure out how to make this profession and skill still work in an upside-down world.

TELL US A LITTLE ABOUT HOW COVID IMPACTED WHAT YOU DO AND HOW YOU ADAPTED

COVID was interesting because it's been both an expanding and contracting of our worlds. If I think about the impact for me personally, as a mediator, when COVID first arrived a lot of us were sitting back staring into our gins wondering what this would mean for the job we do and the profession we love.
Being involved in mostly corporate, commercial mediation, the traditional standard has always been to get everyone into a room, usually for a day, and thrash out the issues, working with people face-to-face to identify whether a resolution is possible. It's true there are lots of forms of mediation that don't always happen in-person but pre-COVID there was a reluctance from many in the industry to step into that space.

So when, all of a sudden, you're told that you can't see anyone outside of your house, let alone fly to a different city to do a mediation with twenty-five lawyers in the room and a whole bunch of parties, your first thought is, *Well I guess that's done.* I didn't know when – or whether, for that matter – it was ever going to come back.

If we put ourselves back into that moment, it's a fascinating thing that happened. Within a couple of days, we were all talking to each other trying to find solutions and saying, 'Okay, how is this going to work?' Not just whether it could be done but also if the market would buy it. We all knew Zoom and various platforms existed and that there were ways we could continue to practice, but we had to figure out how to do it and how to do it effectively. It was great how we all came together, working together, through the basics of how to create break-out rooms, to the deeper questions of, 'How can you build rapport with people through a monitor?' And look at us now, we are all doing that and doing it successfully.

There really was a coming together of people in a lot of different places around the world to share knowledge and share tools about how this new way of working could get us through such difficult times.

Although the dynamics were different, the faces were the same. We've now got more flexibility in bringing people together and a few more tools at our disposal.

TELL US ABOUT DEALING WITH CONFUSION, CONFLICT AND CHANGE SINCE WE'VE BEEN IMPACTED BY COVID

I haven't seen that people are now more willing to resolve their issues, but equally, I don't perceive much more difficulty in resolving conflicts.

I don't know what it was like for others, but here in New

Zealand at the start of COVID, there was an initial 'stop' – a pause, where a lot of things and disputes got pushed away to 'down the track'. This was only a delay as, ultimately, these disputes and contracts had to be resolved and we had to find solutions to get back to work. In New Zealand, at least, as we came out of lockdown, the rules were constantly changing. We were all trying to keep up with the new environment and how this impacted what we did. Interestingly, there was also a bit of a snap back. It was almost, 'Okay, well, that's done. Let's all get back together face-to-face in rooms and get on with it.'

The observation I'd make is that face-to-face remains the preferred mode, but the things we've learned have opened up other options and the potential for blended models. There are now many different opportunities around that traditional model that, I think, are beneficial for us. What we are seeing now is more pre-mediation meetings on Zoom. That's a step forward from what we used to do and certainly a lesson in my practice. I think COVID has accelerated our learning as a profession, certainly the rate of adaption within the mediation field has been quite remarkable.

Wearing my corporate hat, we had to learn how to run a law firm differently. Instead of being in two offices in two cities, we were 250 offices in people's kitchens, bedrooms and lounges. In some sense, our team's response to COVID was just a proof of concept. It forced us to adapt to some emerging technologies and figure out how they can be used now. We haven't gone completely back to 'as it was' but are finding our feet settling into a new equilibrium. We have a variety of different tools now and that forced adaptation opened our eyes. These are probably lessons we should learn, not just in relation to COVID and in relation to business, but in how successful we can be adapting in the face of unexpected challenges. It has the potential to set a new standard

– that we can adapt to big changes, and anything is possible.

Perhaps, what we are all being called to do is to be better mediators in our lives. Isn't that the fundamental thing we do in mediation? We convince people that there is another way, and it is possible to get through conflict by adapting. When I say 'convince', I don't mean convinced through the power of our own advocacy, because that's not our job, but to create an environment where people can unpack what the opportunities might be, test them and consider if there's another option. If you aren't doing this as a mediator, creating that environment and creating the conditions where people can have hope, well, then you're not going to be a mediator for very long.

What I have seen, though, is a lot of exhausted people. Particularly people who own and manage businesses, who have had to be 'switched on' for the last two and a half years. People who have been running a business and responsible for other people's jobs and lives. These people are yet to have a break. Their reserves of emotional energy are utterly depleted. And that goes for the mediators as well as the parties and the lawyers and everyone else who's involved in the ecosystem of any particular conflict.

SHARE YOUR HACKS, INNOVATIONS OR LEARNINGS THAT HAVE EMERGED FROM THIS TIME

I guess one of the learnings for me has been the emerging flexibility that COVID has pushed us into. We are dealing with similar conflicts, similar people, but now we have more tools to deal with the issues. We've got more flexibility to bring people together. That is really exciting for the dispute resolution industry and great for our clients.

There is one standout hack for me during this period, which

might sound really basic, but has had a big impact, and that is to describe to people the environment I'm working in. Because literally everyone relates to body language cues online but understanding where we are placed and what is happening around us has helped me manage assumptions and reduce the risk of negative interpretations. I will now always explicitly describe what my desk looks like. For instance, 'You're on a screen on my laptop in front of me, and up here on my right is a screen that has all my documents on it. And if you see me looking over there, I'm not daydreaming, I'm not reading anything else. That's where the documents are.' It is about locating people in that space, and it was one of the most useful things I learned to do.

I'm also seeking a hack and I'm 'throwing it out to the crowd'. In face-to-face mediation work, there are always moments of interaction that occur between rooms, as we walk next to people, or by the 'water cooler'. I do a lot of my work in the nooks and crannies of the mediation moving between rooms with people. The challenge for me has been to find a way to do that when we're all online. I did a mediation last week where one of the parties said something in open session and I was really taken aback by it. And the other side was surprised to. I was able to deal with this challenge as I was walking alongside the person's lawyer saying, 'Hey, can you please help out with the process and have a chat with [*that person*], because she's not being helpful.' How do you do that in an online zone? Just send them a private chat? Invariably, I'll send that chat to 'everybody' and that puts the whole mediation at risk. You can't have that sort of quiet fireside chat over a text or a chat message. I suppose the corporate word for it would be, 'how do you replace the watercooler conversation?'

TELL US ABOUT THE CRAICS, CROCODILE TEARS AND STANDOUT MOMENTS FROM THE LAST FEW YEARS

A standout for me over this time has been how willing most people have been to try and make things work. At least for a little while, there was a great margin of appreciation for the fact that we're all trying to figure out how to fly the plane while we're still building it. Nothing's gone completely pear-shaped, but there have certainly been funny moments along the way.

I think this goes back to the work we did as professionals in small groups of professional learning. Learning how to do this and sharing knowledge; sharing some of those tips about how the system works, how to go about signing a document, what you can you do if someone can't print something. For me, it was a group of us who came together to talk through things and find solutions. We pulled together a few fellow mediators that we knew across Australia and New Zealand, and we gathered on Zoom nearly every week, initially. As time went on, it stretched out to two weeks, a month and now even longer. We set aside an hour with a drink of our choice, and just talked and listened to where we were all at. I remember conversations that I had individually and as a part of the group, and I really enjoyed it. It was immensely valuable to figure stuff out, because we all came at these things from different backgrounds and with different skills, but we were able to pull solutions together. One of the challenges of our mediation profession is that it is intensely individual, and generally in the past, there hasn't been enough exchanging of knowledge and ideas.

The reality is that we are dealing with complex disputes with people and we don't always get things right either; we are human, after all. In the past we would dust ourselves off, get back up and move along to the next issue. With COVID we were all experiencing new things and new ideas. It really was a standout to be able to get together with people you can rely on and an opportunity for reflective practice in a way we haven't had traditionally. Having someone to connect with and say, 'I think you did that fine,' or, 'I can see how that went sideways.'

LOOKING FORWARD, WHAT DO YOU THINK MIGHT BE SOME LASTING TRENDS OR INFLUENCES?

The big challenge for us is how we take the best out of everything we've learned and adapt that into what I think is still best practice, which is mostly the face-to-face interaction. What will be most used in my practice are some of the online tools available for pre-mediation meetings. The online environment is fantastic because now I can have more conversations with a party in advance of a mediation. The 'old-fashioned' pre-COVID way of doing this was to talk to the lawyers beforehand. Now we don't have to fly around just to do a pre-mediation. And you get so much gold out of these sessions, being able to do them with the party and the lawyers. Having a frank discussion about a week or two before the mediation is just so valuable!

Here in New Zealand, mediation is relatively advanced in the commercial space, in terms of the acceptability of mediation. Where we are developing is in the idea of recognising the value of the mediation and the skills of the mediator. Not everyone who is a good lawyer can turn their minds to becoming a good mediator. There are a lot of people out there who have done the training, but I think we are at a pivot point in the industry. I'm noticing less demand in the legal market for people wanting evaluative mediation. Instead, there is a bit of a hurricane, with a number of really well-trained mediators, who can mediate a construction dispute, right through to professional indigenous disputes and contractual disputes. These 'good' mediators have a skill set that is adjacent to, but separate and distinct from, being able to understand the legal minutes.

YOUR TIPS FOR DEALING WITH PEOPLE DYNAMICS DURING CONFUSION, CHANGE AND CONFLICT

- Slow down. Appreciate that people in conflict or confusion need more time to process, understand and hear than they would in usual circumstances. This is true for all of us. We may feel pressure to make a quick decision, to react and 'just sort it out'. It is normal to feel this pressure to decide NOW, but by slowing it down, we create space to gather information, reflect and really hear each other.
- Context matters. Be aware that sometimes there are a lot of contributing factors, like COVID stress, that may be happening to you too and you need to account for that. Be gentle on yourself, listen to advice and give yourself a break so you can 'reset' your mental wellbeing.
- Remember that true diplomacy is telling people to 'go to hell' in such a way that they look forward to the trip. Finding a good outcome doesn't have to be 'cardigan wearing, soft or fluffy'. When you are negotiating, sometimes the best way to get what you want is to make them feel like *they* got a 'deal'.

BIO

Hayden is the chairman of Dentons Kensington Swan (formerly Kensington Swan) and plays a key role in the firm's relationships with government agencies. Hayden is a member of the global board of Dentons. Hayden is a dispute resolution expert and is internationally recognised as a leading advocate and as a highly skilled mediator. He has extensive experience helping organisations resolve complex commercial and public law issues.

Hayden works across the range of public law disciplines including core administrative public law issues, advice on legislative obligations and judicial review in the public sector. His public law expertise and networks have led him to be involved in some of the most highly sensitive commercial projects and relationships that the New Zealand Government has been involved in.

He is a strategic thinker with the ability to assess legal, political and reputational risk, having worked with the senior levels of the public sector and the executive for the majority of his career. He helps both public and private sector clients manage a wide range of public law issues, including managing and reviewing risk, advising on privacy and information law, human rights obligations and regulatory issues. Hayden and his team provide crisis management support and advice in relation to government or regulatory investigations, inquiries or prosecutions.

Hayden trained as a mediator through the Resolution Institute in New Zealand, at the Straus Institute for Dispute Resolution at Pepperdine University in California and at Harvard University. He has served as vice-chair of Resolution Institute and is a distinguished fellow of the International Academy of Mediators.

dentons.co.nz

HAYLEY JARICK
A MORE SUSTAINABLE FUTURE

Little things can make a massive difference. If everybody did one little thing, then collectively those little things add up. Collaborating with each other can make an enormous difference on a global and a micro level.

Pre-COVID, everyone was sailing on smooth water in different types and sizes of boats. The COVID storm added incredibly rough seas into the mix. People were people trying to figure out how to battle the new conditions. Boats were sinking. Sometimes they ran into each other. Some ran out of fuel. Sailors couldn't pick which way the wind is blowing, as it came from every direction. In these conditions, it's hard to stay focused on the lighthouse.

TELL US ABOUT WHAT YOU DO AND WHAT YOU LOVE ABOUT WHAT YOU DO?

Primarily my day job is CEO and company secretary of the *Supply Chain Sustainability School Limited*, an Australian not-for-profit entity training people about social, environmental and economic sustainability issues.

As an extension of that, I also do several other things. I'm a director of *Responsible Steel*, a global stewardship scheme and membership community for a group of organisations trying to improve responsible behaviours within the steel industry. That includes improving labour forces, decarbonising production, looking after local communities, and everything in between.

There are also a number of things I love to do and am passionate about. I volunteer with Planet Ark and chair the Australian Circular Economy Hub Circular Procurement Working Group. Circularity is massive now, and I'm happy to be working with them in procurement. I am also volunteering with WWF's *Materials Embodied Carbon Leaders Alliance* (MECLA), a collaboration of organisations trying to reduce the embodied carbon of building materials. So, in that space, I sit on their PCG governance group, and I chair two of their committees; one on steel and one on knowledge sharing and developing a common language.

In my 'spare time', I'm a wife and mum of two and I love my role as scout leader for a mob of Joeys. I'm always looking to see where I can help out in the community, so for a few years now, I've been volunteering as a mentor for people working in non-government organisations and not-for-profit groups.

I wear many hats and like to do different things. I do way too much, but at the end of the day, I can sleep easy knowing I am putting all of my skills and privilege to good use in the world.

It was about ten years ago when I had a wake-up call, and, in that reflection, I realised I like the 'social justice' element of life. From a very young age, I've always believed that if you see something that doesn't feel right, you should stand up for it. And if you have a voice, especially when others don't, I think there's an obligation to speak up for people when they can't. I've made a conscious decision to have conversations with people with different trains of thought and contrasting beliefs to mine. I want to understand where they're coming from, not so I can try to convince them to think the way I do but to find a way to get to a good outcome that we can both live with.

I improved those skills when I worked at the *Resolution Institute*. I had the privilege of working with many people in dispute and conflict resolution, and I could see the pros and cons of viewpoints from multiple personalities, which encouraged me to reflect on how I integrate with others.

TELL ABOUT DEALING WITH CONFUSION, CHANGE AND CONFLICT SINCE WE'VE BEEN IMPACTED BY COVID?

COVID was an interesting time. To give people a little bit of background, the *Supply Chain Sustainability School is* run remotely, so I work from home and always have since I started in the role. It was a critical factor in the position that I had to get used to before COVID. When I started working from home, it was unusual, and there were few people doing it. There weren't many systems and setups in place, but I found my way through it and discovered what worked for me by reaching out to others and doing plenty of research that could help me to run a business remotely. I was always looking for ways to connect with people, and I'm still finding solutions today to achieve that social interaction. I had done all that a few years ago, and when COVID came along, everyone moved into working from home very quickly. Suddenly, people were facing that isolation for the first time. I had many people asking, 'How do you do it?' But I was no longer the expert on working from home because all my coping mechanisms weren't available to me either. The things I would do to clear my head, like walking around the block, I couldn't do. I was fine working from home in isolation, but suddenly, I had my husband and kids at home with me as well. It was a different office environment. I still had to adapt while trying to share what I had learnt with other people.

At the same time, professionally, because we were an online school with a lot of online material ready to go, work took off, and I was swamped. We had many people coming online when they weren't comfortable using online services. The dynamic and culture of the people we were serving was utterly different once COVID hit. We went from people who were high-tech and would do most of their learning on their commute to work or from their office in the morning, to people who were utterly computer illiterate. We had to write frequently asked question responses on how to log in. Err…. you hit the Login button. Or 'How do I reset the password?' You hit the 'Forgot My Password' button. We never even thought we'd have to write an instruction guide on how to do that because we thought it was apparent. So for a time, it was a massive workload with the changing dynamic of people coming online and doing things differently. We had to recalibrate how we communicated with everyone at a time when we knew people were stressed. Half the workforce was trying to do things they'd never done before, but with no help.

When you're overworked, trying to reframe the whole conversation and be empathetic is hard. You want to say, 'What kind of idiot doesn't know how to reset their password?' Right? These days, we all look at that and know what to do, but for everyone at the time, I understood why some people weren't used to that stuff. It's hard not to sound condescending when you say you 'hit the reset password button' because they might have been looking at it for thirty minutes, but you don't want them to feel stupid about it.

The way people were learning was utterly different. We had to flip our entire operation from one-hour-long e-learning modules, which was the pinnacle of online learning, to sometimes just two minutes. Ten minutes was the longest course anyone would ever do - two minutes perfect. We were trying to cater to every learning style, so we had to flip everything to be more videos, more podcasts, more interactive learning, and short, sharp infographics. Suddenly, people were learning in between other things. They wanted to be able to stop and start on demand when they needed to because they might be watching, and the kids would need attention. It was a whole different world and dynamic that people were operating in. Everything familiar changed; how they shopped, the type of food they could buy, and things they'd done the same every day for years. The comfort factors that bring you stability and you'd put on repetition your whole life were suddenly gone.

Ten years ago, you'd go into the office, and if one person had a bad day, you could rally and support them. During COVID, every single person in the office was having a bad day at the same time, and you never knew, even five seconds before you joined a Zoom call, exactly what was going on. It was a high-pressure situation. At the same time, there was a fantastic amount of positives to take from it. People I'd only met online during the lockdown and whom I got to know so well, when we finally met in person, it was hard to believe we'd not previously met face to face. We'd been on the same team and had meetings with their laundry in the background. We'd met their children, their families, and their pets, and seen pretty much every nook and cranny of the house as they walked around trying to find a quiet spot to chat while they were on Zoom. I knew what their bookshelf and their backyard looked like and all that sort of information because we were all in a bizarre environment. It's that sort of thing that lets you know people on a different level.

Another change that happened was that all of the introverts came out. Typically, we used to run many workshops in large environments; massive conferences with hundreds of people in the room. They were big workshops where we encouraged people to speak openly and stand up in front of groups and talk. It was an extrovert's heaven and hell if you're an introvert. It would take an introvert the whole day to build enough energy to go to an event like that. I think introverts would have loved how everybody worked in the COVID world, while the extroverts struggled to adapt themselves to an introverted environment.

For me, COVID shone a light on the fact that I'm a borderline introvert/extrovert. Every time I've done assessments, I've been right in the middle, and I've always known that about myself. The amount I learned about myself and others working through the COVID situation was insane because of the intensity it placed on social dynamics.

TELL US ABOUT THE CRAICS, CROCODILE TEARS AND STANDOUT MOMENTS FROM THE LAST FEW YEARS?

Regarding the work I do daily, we train people through supply chains on different social, environmental and economic issues.

We talk to people and companies involved in the supply chains of big organisations who are tackling, for example, their 'modern slavery eradication processes', and we're upskilling the whole network so suppliers can figure out, 'what is modern slavery?' and 'how do we look out for it?' When we first start talking about this, most people ask, 'why are you talking about something that happened 200 years ago?' Most importantly, we're looking at breaking that trend of ignorance to provide information about how it's still happening. During the conversation, everyone has a moment when the reality sinks in, and they are appalled. They go from denial to feeling overwhelmed and helpless about how to resolve these issues. The same thing happens with every topic we deal with. If we talk about climate change and how to reduce your carbon footprint or water security and how we can improve water quality storage or recycling and how that all works, everyone goes through the same emotional journey. It's usually a classic 'grief' response. It always starts with denial, 'that's ridiculous; that's not even a problem.' Once you get through that, there's anger, then acceptance.

One of the challenging issues is that the people I speak to have a highly varied degree of education. I've got PhDs at the top of the spectrum and people who can't read or speak English at the bottom. How do you try and teach everybody in that range about modern slavery? And it can be even more complex because someone may have a PhD in a completely different field. For example, they could have a PhD in an environmental field and I'm training them about modern slavery. It's often hard to get someone who is extremely intelligent in what they know to step back and recognise that they are ignorant of something else. They often feel they don't need the training, 'I can figure this out for myself.'

So getting back to the conflict aspects in that process, it's dealing with everyone individually and trying to understand where they're coming from, appreciating the diversity and trying to be as inclusive as possible, while moving everyone along – just one step. There's sometimes an immense pressure to try and fix everything or solve everything rather than moving forward, one step at a time. That's the goal of each session, to take one step in the right direction without trying to fix everything right there and then because that's never going to work. And because of the overwhelm of COVID, it was even more important to break it down into that one step.

To give you a picture of what my day-to-day felt like during COVID, I'm going to use sailing as an analogy. Pre-COVID, everyone was sailing on smooth water. We all had different size boats with different technologies, some were sailing, and some had motors, but the water was smooth, and we just wanted to find our way around. COVID added incredibly rough seas into the mix, so not only were people trying to figure out how to battle the rough seas in whatever boat they had chosen, but sometimes the boats were sinking, sometimes they ran into each other, or were running out of gas. Trying to pick which way the wind is blowing, when it's coming from every direction, is hard. Then I'm sitting there like a lighthouse in the storm, saying, 'please try and think about climate change.' Everyone is saying, 'that's great, I'd love to focus on the lighthouse and get there, but I've got so much other stuff to deal with first.'

I do think there's been an increasing awareness of social justice and sustainability principles during COVID, as it has forced a significant percentage of the population to have mini-epiphanies where people are asking themselves, 'If I were to get sick and die tomorrow, would I be happy with what I've done so far?' because suddenly that was a possibility. The things that seemed important pre-COVID might not be so important anymore. What might now be relevant is, 'what is truly important to me?' Pre-COVID, we all looked at our standard risk assessment matrix with different eyes. The risk of a hundred-year flood - low probability. The threat of a global pandemic – low likelihood. But all of a sudden, these things happened and had massive consequences. The systems we used to evaluate these very complex issues before seemed utterly irrelevant. This whole world of consequence and likelihood of risk assessment, even if you never did it that formally, has been turned upside down.

It's forced everyone to sit back and think about what's important. We could clearly see the links between the environmental aspects of what's happening and our health. When the traffic stopped, and all the smog disappeared because people stopped using combustible fossil fuels, they were suddenly able to breathe, and the air was cleaner.

There were so many stories from around the world that forced people to sit back and have those conversations. I wasn't at all surprised as we moved through COVID, especially from an Australian context, that we have so many people changing jobs. When work dropped out, we suddenly valued cleaners and supermarket workers much more highly. And conversations included, 'if we think cleaning is essential, then why are we not making sure that our cleaners are being looked after and paid properly?' All these sorts of questions start to pop out, and we begin empathising with other people's occupations. We need to value the skills that people have in different spaces.

I developed more faith in humanity because people were forced to react. What I found heart-warming were things like when we had international students whose day jobs shut down, but they didn't qualify for welfare and were quite literally starving because they couldn't work to get money. They didn't have money to feed themselves or pay their bills. As soon as everyone knew that problem was happening, an equal amount of people were willing to go out there and cook meals and donate their time to hand them out to perfect strangers to make sure they survived. Stories like that give me incredible hope for humanity. It can get a little depressing for everyone working in the sustainability space when you're constantly dealing with eradicating modern slavery, mitigating climate change and trying to prevent biodiversity loss. You understand the science and can see the devastation that's coming, but you can't get anyone to take action and change because it's so mentally hard to deal with. But when you start to see there are people out there willing to put their hand in their pocket and step up to make someone's day a little bit joyous by something as simple as cooking a meal, it gives me hope for humanity.

Pre-COVID, for many companies, there was much talk around tackling changes that needed to happen. Still, there were many barriers to addressing environmental and social issues making it feel 'just too hard'.

Then suddenly, during COVID, everyone saw how fast organisations could move when needed; working from the cloud, no longer having to travel to a central location and sit at a desk for eight hours. All of these issues were challenged, and very quickly, we were able to adapt, finding resolutions to make it work. That experience gave people a greater sense of challenging other areas where they've also been told, 'no, it's too hard'.

So within that, many other social issues popped up that we began to challenge. It's no longer ok to say, 'it's too hard to hire women in this space,' or 'we've got long-standing supplier relationships we need to nurture; we can't upset them.' Now that the whole supply chain has been disrupted, why not try a social procurement strategy? Why not try buying from an indigenous supplier? Why not source from multiple places instead of one single place?

Why can't we open up that visibility to the entire supply chain? COVID has made everyone more knowledgeable about where our raw materials come from. And understanding this, we are more aware of the risks in our supply chain. There are many people in procurement starting to have conversations around, not just 'how on earth do I get this here?' but 'while everything's up in the air, if we're going to change anything, and disrupt the supply channel, now's a good time to do it!'

Similarly, when you start talking about other environmental issues, peoples' experiences have changed. It's noticeable in our field of vision that with industry shutting down, there was less air and water pollution, so people are now starting to challenge why we've always done things a certain way and question what can be done to make improvements. 'Is there another way of doing things?'

A trend I'm seeing is that employers are challenged in having an engaged workforce. They have to push for employment with a purpose. It's no longer about throwing money at someone, as it's very much an employee's market out there. Corporations are now realising that having transparency and credibility towards environmental and sustainability targets is driving and attracting the top of the employee pool to work for them. If you want the 'best' people to be working for you, you have to have a stand on this.

You'd be hard-pressed to find an award-winning company, one of the top employers with the happiest workforce, who doesn't have a carbon zero target or a stance on something environmental or social. We're seeing a rise in companies asking, 'what can we do to try and make people happy at a micro level?' That's when we're starting to give individuals the flexibility to find things that are important to them. Whether that's having flexible Friday mornings so they can go and read to their kids at school or on Thursday afternoons coaching a soccer team or netball team, people are starting to find a balance in big macro issues like climate change and human rights, but also at an absolute micro level, and touching base on that to round themselves out holistically around finding fulfilment in volunteering. You don't necessarily have to pay people more, but give them the flexibility to do that. That's the happiness people are seeking. So from that corporate point of view, there's a lot of change and sparks on everything at the macro and micro level.

SHARE YOUR HACKS, INNOVATIONS, OR LEARNINGS THAT HAVE EMERGED FROM THIS TIME?

I have four points that are relevant here.
- Find learning in everything. One of the most memorable assignments I completed when I was doing my MBA was to read a book, anything we wanted, then find a way to relate it to something that was course-related and how that could improve our work life. What it meant was that everyone was finding some learning in everything. Even when you watch a movie or read a biography, you learn things you never expected about different lifestyles and how you might be able to adapt that to your life. Just be intensely curious about how cultures operate and things work in different areas, then take that learning and adapt it back to something that relates to you. Read, watch, do something completely random, and then see if you can apply that to your everyday life.

- Explore having a mindful experience outside of your comfort zone. COVID has taught us that even though doing something 'different' is scary, we always learn from it. Most people would probably spend their life trying not to push themselves too far out of their comfort zone because it's where they feel safe and confident. They feel like they're in control. But when you push yourself outside of your comfort zone in a safe environment, you can learn, grow and adapt. And I say 'mindful experience' because it's essential to understand that you're going to go through an emotional journey as you do something different. You're going to feel anxious and awkward. You'll feel incapable and sometimes completely incompetent about what you're doing. And that's completely fine. I would never trade all my most horrible moments because I learned so much from them. Yes, there could have been an easier way to learn those lessons, but I would never want to erase any of those from my history because of what I have learned from them.

    And I say 'mindful experience' because it's essential to understand that you're going to go through an emotional journey as you do something different. You're going to feel anxious and awkward. You'll feel incapable and sometimes completely incompetent about what you're doing. And that's completely fine.

- Fail something – learn to live with failure. That probably sounds odd because we're pushed in our society to be perfect. We put up our best selves on social media, gloss a cover over it and hope we get lots of likes. And that's what validates us for being great people. Then we go to work and try to be perfect at everything we do. We like it when everything goes to plan. We live in this world of constant affirmation of greatness. And yet, failure is such a balancing part of that world. I think you should fail often; if you're not failing, you're not trying often enough, learning to live with failure and learning to admit when you've made a mistake or an error is a most humbling thing. There is a sense of absolute ownership when you realise you've made a mistake, just to say, 'you know what, I'm wrong. I'm sorry. Let me see if I can fix that.'

Especially when you're working with people in high-stress environments, being able to be fallible at one thing doesn't necessarily make you vulnerable. It makes you more confident and credible as you go in for the next step. Because if people can understand that you're willing to admit when you're wrong when you hold your ground and say, 'No, I'm right,' they may be more inclined to listen.

You can't be courageous if there's no fear, and you can't appreciate success if you have never failed. It's easy to say that people are good and evil, but there is a myriad of grey in between. There's a little bit of superhero and villain in every one of us. We are all a little bit superhero and a little villain sometimes. So, admitting you're a little bit villain can give you clarity. And then, of course, that gives you the courage to say proudly, ' today, I was a little bit superhero.'

- Do something today. If you have a great idea, there's no reason for anything to hold you back but fear. Fear of the unknown or a million excuses you'll come up with as to why you can't do it. But if you do one thing today, and break the inertia, it could make a world of difference. From a sustainability perspective, if you're a Procurement Manager, you can say, 'I'm changing the policy'. And anyone else, in either a business or at home, can do that too. You can make a personal choice in your buying habits to say, 'you know what! I'm not going to buy anything new for three months, and just see if I can make do with what I've got.

Or if I need something, I'm going to buy it second-hand.'

Just making one different choice the next time you go grocery shopping, like checking if the packaging can be recycled or eating one more meat-free meal a week, can have a massive impact on your carbon footprint. You could even ask the question when you buy things if there is a chance that someone has been involved in modern slavery in the production of those goods or services. Little things can make a massive difference. If everybody did one little thing, then collectively those little things add up. Collaborating with each other can make an enormous difference on a global and a micro level.

LOOKING FORWARD, WHAT DO YOU THINK MIGHT BE SOME LASTING TRENDS OR INFLUENCES?

There's an ongoing trend towards transparency. Through COVID, we've increased our transparency significantly with things like supply chain agreements., Or even just understanding how logistics work. I think that's going to grow as we move forward.

Being transparent is about being fully open and disclosing anything you have done or what you may have seen. It's time to be transparent; if you don't admit it, someone else will find out and tell the world anyway. We've recently had many cases of assault in the workplace, and I think getting on the front foot and reporting that being proactive about trying to find resolution in those areas, is going to be massive. Similarly, around areas where you might not have direct responsibility, like talking about modern slavery, people are becoming more aware of their supply chains and investigating these areas. When you find or suspect that there's a case of modern slavery in your supply chain, in your office, or your car park, speak up. There are plenty of examples of this happening in Australia. It's a myth that this is only happening overseas. There are 1000s of people in Australia currently living in modern slavery. To keep our finger on the pulse about that, becoming more transparent will not only force people to disclose in that area, but then they can work through a process on exactly how to remediate the issues

There is also a trend for more collaboration, Universally, people are starting to see that you can't do everything on your own. Individually, you can't be all things to all people and solve everything for everyone. You have to partner with others to make that happen. And you're better off not partnering with duplicates of yourself but with people or organisations who have a different perspective. Increased diversity of thought, age, race, physical ability, neurodiversity, and religion; collaborating with those people is going to increase your thought spectrum and reduce risk. Work with others to fill the gaps in your weaknesses, and get things done. I also see a lot more purpose-driven collaborations between companies in terms of sustainability, environment and social justice.

Those trends for transparency and collaboration, are going to generate real outcomes from corporates in the near future.

YOUR TIPS FOR DEALING WITH PEOPLE DYNAMICS DURING CONFUSION, CHANGE AND CONFLICT

- Learn to be mindful. That's a massive personal journey everyone can go on. Physically, we take care of our body with exercise and healthy food so that when we need to, we can endure, sprint, lift and react to protect ourselves from harm. When we are hurt, we seek the help of medical professionals, like doctors and physiotherapists, to aid in our recovery.

We need to treat our minds like we do our physical bodies. Exercising our minds and learning to be mindful is essential. We can learn to recognise when we're having emotional reactions to things, like being happy, sad, angry or anxious. Being mindful and knowing that your body is going through those different emotions is an essential step on a journey to emotional intelligence.

- Be kind to yourself. You can't be everything to everybody all the time. And similarly, you can't resolve everything. Sometimes you may be a part of the dispute, and you may need a third party to help resolve it. It doesn't mean you failed. It doesn't mean you're not smart. It doesn't mean that you are not experienced. It is what it is. You don't have to be the conflict resolver, best friend, wife, boss, colleague, and everything in one. That is impossible. Be kind to yourself and let somebody else take some of the burden.
- Celebrate the small things. Discover what brings you joy and just celebrate it. Celebrate when you finish the test, not just when you get the results. Even if it's just 'yay, it's Friday….I lived another week.' As a small example, my daughter loves to tell jokes, and during the lockdown she found her favourite jokes, and I helped her to print them out. We put them on our front fence and as everyone was doing their 'government endorsed' daily walks around the block, people would walk past and read them and chuckle, or not. It formed a bit of a habit, and even though we didn't realise it at the time, it brought us joy. We had to read 1000 jokes to find five good ones. And I'd be sitting in my office, and people would walk past the front and randomly burst out laughing. Of course, then I would smile. It's those little milestones – you never really know the impact that will have on somebody else.

A guy was walking past with his dog recently, when my son ran out in his karate uniform, and jumped into a car. The guy said, 'I never know what's going to pop out at me when I'm walking my dog, but I sure didn't expect a ninja to run in front of me and get taken away in a car!' We both laughed, and I thought, 'what a funny thing to make his day.' Then a little way up the road, he turned and said, 'Oh, by the way, when are you bringing back the jokes?' We had stopped the jokes at the end of lockdown, but it was wonderful to celebrate that a stranger had their day brightened by one small act.

BIO

As CEO and company secretary for Supply Chain Sustainability School, Hayley leads a charity committed to leading Australian and Aotearoa New Zealand industries into a more sustainable future by developing sustainability competence in the supply chain. Hayley has extensive experience in governance, strategic management, marketing, membership, adult learning, advocacy, financial analytics, sales and customer service in manufacturing, residential and commercial building, heavy construction, professional services and international trade; for-profit and for-purpose; big and small; paid and voluntary. She is currently an independent director for ResponsibleSteel and is chair for the Australian Circular Economy Hub Circular Procurement Working Group, amongst other volunteer roles.

linkedin.com/in/hayleyjarick

HAZEL HERRINGTON
WE RISE TOGETHER

COVID forced me to walk an internal conflict about who I am and how I care for me. But it also forced me to adapt my business model and create something that could weather unpredictability.

Everyone needs an mediator in their back pocket, someone who can help them better navigate the conflict in their lives.

TELL US ABOUT WHAT YOU DO AND WHAT YOU LOVE ABOUT WHAT YOU DO

I'm the founder and CEO of Herrington Publications Worldwide (HPW). HPW is a publishing company specialising in books and magazines that help women, entrepreneurs and global leaders to build powerful and strong brands. We offer our clients a range of services to reach their goals, including virtual and in-person events, marketing plans and strategies, and one-on-one consultations.

I'm often taken aback by the transformations my clients undergo when they start working with us. Most come to me curious about how we will help them grow their brand in such a short time frame.

After months of hard work, developing content, engaging audiences on social media platforms and participating in podcasts or webinars, it's amazing to witness the transformation from a shy entrepreneur to a confident leader. Every day I see successful individuals who have been birthed from HPW's powerful network of resources. It's inspiring to know that through our efforts, we are helping people reach new heights in their professional development journey.

At HPW we strive to provide the best possible service to our clients through persistent dedication and cutting-edge techniques. We create custom marketing plans tailored specifically for each client's needs while ensuring that our practices remain up to date with the latest industry trends. Through our comprehensive approach, we are proud to have established ourselves as a leading source for personal brand development among women entrepreneurs worldwide.

TELL US A LITTLE ABOUT HOW COVID IMPACTED WHAT YOU DO AND HOW YOU ADAPTED

Herrington Publications Worldwide would not exist without

COVID, so there are many advantages as well as the disadvantages that came with COVID. When it hit Australia, I was pushed into a corner. I was running an events company, and suddenly we couldn't hold in-person events anymore. The reality for me, and many others, was that prior to COVID, we spent possibly 25% of our time online with our business. With COVID, we were suddenly spending all our time online. I was forced to adapt and make big changes to survive. So, I shifted my business model and birthed Herrington Publications. The focus was magazine publications and coaching, as well as publishing books and magazines.

As a single mum, it has been tough. There have been losses in income along with the time and funding I've had to put into this new business, but I am so proud to be empowering women. And perhaps, most importantly, while there have certainly been moments of conflict, I am confident that I will now be able to sustainably provide for my daughter. And having managed to do this successfully, I am now able to share my story with others. I know there are people out there who have been traumatised because of the impact of COVID, and those who have perhaps lost businesses. COVID's biggest impact though has generally been on our mental health, and I want to be able to let everyone know, that even if you lose everything, you can start again.

It certainly hasn't been easy. It came at a very high cost for me, and I found myself completely burnt-out. I know that I am not alone in this but I had to do the hard work. I had to come up with a daily strategy of how I was going to cope. One of the things I did during this time was invest in personal development. Not just professional development, but personal development, and I learnt to prioritise my mental health. A massive learning from this time is that you have to take care of your health, mentally and physically. If you're not going to get up and look after *you*, then nothing will change.

Whether you believe in the Bible, whether you believe in yoga, in meditation or something else, I believe that every morning needs a routine. Make time to pray, worship or do something for your mental health. It could be as simple as exercise or going for a walk, but have a daily routine so that you are motivated and encouraged.

COVID forced me to work on my internal conflict about who I am and how I care *for me*. But it also forced me to adapt my business model and create something that could weather the storm of unpredictability.

TELL US ABOUT DEALING WITH CONFUSION, CHANGE AND CONFLICT SINCE WE'VE BEEN IMPACTED BY COVID

Throughout COVID, I've had the privilege of working closely with businesswomen and entrepreneurs from across the world; women who are trying to make a difference and secure financial freedom for themselves and their families. But through that time, I also noticed that there were three types of women.

The first type were women who decided they were going sit back and watch what was going to happen. I wasn't one of those women.

Then there were women, like myself, who decided, *I'm going to do something about this, I'm not going to be a victim*. These were the women who decided to put themselves out there. They have worked to overcome their fears. Everyone feels fear, it's just some people let fear stop them and others use it to push forward.

It was these women who had the courage to create a new idea and then put it into action. These were the women who consistently said, 'How are we going to innovate?'

Then there was a third group of women, they started and ran with us, but then they gave up. They gave up when the going got tough.

When I reflect on this, I realise that conflict was behind so much of this, and we each deal with those conflicts differently, the internal and external conflict.

Sadly, over this time, I have also seen a lot of conflict with women online; women who were competing in similar or even different markets, women who would attack and undermine others if they thought they were doing well. However, we don't talk about this. We don't show how much it hurts. Ladies, please pay attention – you will always come cross paths with someone who is intimidated by your success. Some women will clap and celebrate with you, some women will retreat from you and wonder why they are missing out, and some women will work to bring you down.

These experiences have taught me that if you are going to operate a business online, you need to understand that not everyone is going to like you. There will be haters, there will be passive-aggressive attacks and not everyone will buy your products. You need to be strong. If you are stepping up to be a global entrepreneur, it takes double the strength. Therefore, I do all I can to support women who take the risk and run with it.

I see conflict resolution skills as critical to women in business, especially those who spend the majority of time online. It can be hard to know what to do. How do we solve these issues and how do we navigate these 'people' problems when they impact us? Often, despite getting emotional, we pretend everything is okay. Usually, we try to do it all on our own. I think, now more than ever, we need to be confident enough to ask for help from professionals who understand conflict and what it can do to business. What I've learnt from Sarah, a conflict strategist, are simple techniques that support my mental health in this area, like picking your battles, blocking or just ignoring. Honestly, I don't have time for drama. I wonder if perhaps part of the impact of COVID, being so much stress and confusion, has led some people to put their energy into bringing others down. It's their way of dealing with the stress. While the rest of us are too busy making a real difference.

TELL US ABOUT THE CRAICS, CROCODILE TEARS AND STANDOUT MOMENTS FROM THE LAST FEW YEARS

I'll tell you about my lowest moment during COVID. My eldest daughter was at university in the United Kingdom, and I got a call saying she had been in a domestic violence situation and was in hospital. I just cried. I couldn't be there for her, and I cried and cried. Before COVID, I could have jumped on a flight and been there in a day. But now I couldn't. We talked on the phone, but it just wasn't good enough. My heart goes out to those who lost family members and were separated from their families, unable to go to funerals or weddings. I know that feeling of separation. It has been so hard for so many of us.

But there have been amazing moments too. For me, it was getting together with family online. It took some time teaching the oldies how to use Zoom, setting things up and coordinating the process, but we got there eventually, and it was so wonderful – all of us on Zoom, laughing, joking, cracking jokes. We found a way to come together. I look back and still laugh at those funny moments with my grandmothers and aunties, it was just crazy. I remember my mum being on mute and we could see she was talking the whole time, but of course we couldn't hear her. We tried telling her she was muted, but it was just so funny.

And honestly, as a mum, it became very clear to me that I am NOT a teacher. I love my daughter and I love that she was learning, but she would come to me with homework for me to do and I had to learn it myself before I could teach her! I was able to do the mathematics on the iPad, and English and reading was okay – but everything else, sorry, it just wasn't happening. Plus, our kids don't listen to us, they don't take us seriously as teachers. I look back and laugh. I really must salute the teachers; they've got so much patience. I am so very grateful that she is back at school.

SHARE YOUR HACKS, INNOVATIONS OR LEARNINGS THAT HAVE EMERGED FROM THIS TIME

Prepare, prepare, prepare – don't wing it. Preparation time is never wasted time. Whatever you are doing, make the time to prepare. I'm talking from experience when I say I've seen so many people who come on stage or arrive at an interview without having done any preparation. We can see this lack of preparation, you know – don't think we don't notice.

Every morning I prepare for my day. I do this as it helps me mentally and spiritually to be able to do the work I do. There is routine and structure. I get up early when everything is quiet, and I worship. That's my thing, and I am not ashamed of it. There is too much conflict and judgement about what each of us does and how. Find your own thing, whatever it is, and bring that discipline to your preparation, for your day, your project or your talk – wherever it is you want to make a difference.

Boundaries – during this time, I have also had to examine and reassess my boundaries. My burnout forced me to reflect on what matters and how I care for myself. I've hired more staff to work with me (mostly virtually), and it's because I want to ensure I make time for me and my family. Whilst I am driven to be successful and grow my influence, it means nothing if I lose my capacity to be present with my daughter. So, learning boundaries by separating work time and family time is critical. In the past when someone wanted to reach out and collaborate with me, we would have a face-to-face meeting. Now I don't do that. Now I value me and my time differently. If I don't know you, and you want to collaborate with me on a project, you're going to send me an agenda first and only if that makes sense, we can meet. I don't meet just anyone. Now I am creating better boundaries, I don't have time to meet everyone.

LOOKING FORWARD, WHAT DO YOU THINK MIGHT BE SOME LASTING TRENDS OR INFLUENCES?

I think we have all had to reassess what matters to us. Success at all costs is no longer okay. We are recognising the importance of family and balancing that with the need for financial freedom. For myself, I prioritise flexibility and choice. Yes, I need financial stability, but it has to be in a way that enables me to be present for my daughter. The high cost of COVID, lives lost, separations, lost businesses and jobs have all forced us to re-evaluate what matters, what success looks like and who we surround ourselves with.

What financial freedom looks like has also changed. Whether you are in business or are employed, it is clear we must be looking to make wise decisions. This means owning our money decisions, whether it is investing, diversifying or whatever it is you choose to do, own those decisions. Seek advice from experts and make decisions that will look forward for sustainability.

How we influence has also changed. We have all had to spend so much time online, we are now using it differently. It isn't about being everywhere and on every platform, much like prioritising our family, we also learning to be smarter about what platforms we use and why. To be strategic about this, you must be clear on what you are working towards. I do think that the future requires us to think differently, less reactively and with more depth. We must all make sure we educate ourselves better and inform ourselves – and with a focus on safety.

What I find interesting too, is that women are stepping out of the victim role. As a migrant woman from Africa, I know that culture has an impact on my beliefs. We are trained to honour and respect our husbands, even if we are being mentally and physically abused. But thankfully, that is changing, though sadly, the change is often driven by trauma. I know of a family who have contracted AIDS because of the cultural advice they were given to stay with the man. 'Oh, you know, that's how men are.' Now these women are dying. I'm so happy to see a shift in how women are stepping up and using their voice, and that's why I continue to go back to Africa to empower those women, and why I work so hard to empower women here, because we are no longer victims. I say to the women I work with, 'You cannot remain a victim and keep going through domestic violence and abuse.' I know in Africa it's still a big problem, especially southern Africa. South African women are being killed. We are so tired of losing women to this pandemic and to gender violence. I think a lot of women are now rising up.

YOUR TIPS FOR DEALING WITH PEOPLE DYNAMICS DURING CONFUSION, CHANGE AND CONFLICT

- Take time out. Dealing with conflict and change takes energy and time. When we don't prioritise ourselves, we pay the cost. Whether it is burnout, broken relationships or something else, the cost is often too high. So, take some time out to rest, care for and value yourself.

    I hope that COVID has reminded us that success is not just about money. Success will mean different things for each of us, but if the cost along the way is the relationships with those that mean the most to us, then somewhere the balance is out.

    Find your thing, prepare yourself for your day – pray,

mediate, exercise, whatever it looks like for you, and find that inner peace.
- Work with an expert. Don't try and do things by yourself. I wasted a lot of time and money trying to do everything myself. I was forced to take a long hard look at myself and recognise that I was getting in my own way. In trying to do it all myself I was slowing myself down.

   If we want to get to a destination fast, we catch a flight. Yes, we could drive, but it will take a long time, there will be more risks, and while we might get there eventually, we'll be exhausted!

   So, invest in a coach and an expert to help you navigate conflict and change. Invest in a team to help share the load.
- The power of collaboration. I feel so strongly about this and need to share and say that collaboration is important for us all. We all have the potential to serve billions of entrepreneurs, clients and communities out there. Too often I find myself speaking to people who say, 'I don't want to collaborate with them, they may steal my idea,' but the reality is that even if they do take your idea, it will never be what you were going to do. We each do things differently and have so much to offer.

   When we collaborate, we share our skills, knowledge and experience to help lift ourselves and others, and in doing this, we all rise. So, reach out, don't be afraid to ask. Email, collaborate, network. Don't be afraid. Reach out to whoever you want to work with. What's the worst thing they can say? If they say no, at least you'll know where you stand, and you can move on in another direction. I have absolutely loved collaborating with so many different women from across the world. It just shows that we can have fun in business, and I have been enjoying myself.

   Ladies, be bold. Be courageous. And reach out through your fear.

BIO

Hazel Herrington is one of the world's leading marketing and personal branding experts. With years of experience developing successful strategies for C-suite executives, entrepreneurs, speakers, authors, coaches and businesses of all sizes. She is the editor-in-chief of publications such as *Lady Politico Power, Lady Speaker Power* and *I Am Woman Global* magazine. Hazel is also a celebrity interviewer who has worked with a list of celebrities, global leaders, politicians, billionaires, millionaires and influencers.

Hazel is a multi-award-winning entrepreneur who has won and been nominated for the following awards: 2021 Most Successful Woman in the World; World Greatness Honorary Award;Gold Coast Woman of the year Award; Australia Top 100 Women of Influence Year; 2021 Exemplary Leadership Award; and the Pan African Thrive global award.

When she's not working, Hazel enjoys spending time with her family, travelling and exploring new places. Hazel holds a bachelor's degree in business from Griffith University and is passionate about helping others succeed.

linkedin.com/in/dr-hazel-herrington
herringtonpublications.com

JOANNE MCMULLAN
DEVELOPING CHANGE RESILIENCE

A big part of dealing with conflict and change is understanding that change is constant. It requires a mindset shift. The truth is that if you're not changing, you're not evolving, you are standing still and you will get left behind. The trick is learning how to manage the conversations around change. This is a skill that many people haven't developed.

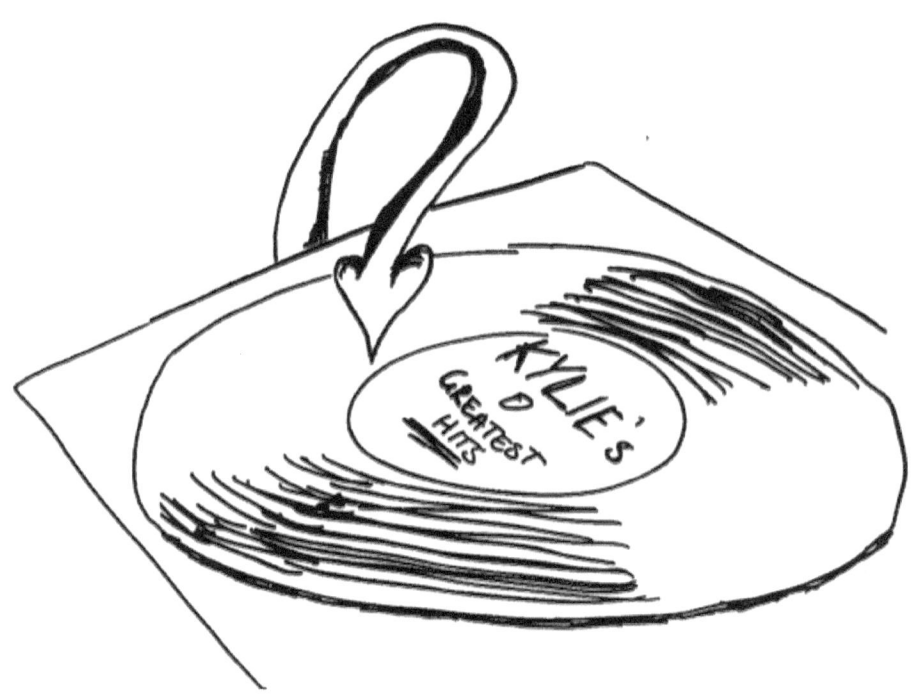

I have a saying I picked up from a book I once read, 'Drop the Kylie!' It's in reference to the song 'Better the Devil You Know' by Kylie Minogue, implying that *the devil you know* isn't better, and in fact, we must 'drop this'.

TELL US ABOUT WHAT YOU DO AND WHAT YOU LOVE ABOUT WHAT YOU DO

Born and raised in Derry, Northern Ireland, conflict was part of life. I've been a resident in Dublin for the last twenty-six years, and like most people, there has been lots of change to deal with in life. I proudly work for an Irish multinational software organisation FINEOS as their chief people officer. I joined them a few years after startup. We are now global across ten countries with 1,200 people onboard from all different walks and stages of life; being part of that growth journey meant continuous transformation for the company and in my career. Our company purpose is to 'help our customers care for the people they serve through the delivery of superior insurance technology'. We are part of the ecosystem, a lifeboat support. We help our customers serve people who suffer illness, injury or loss and are dealing with all the difficult things life throws their way. My job, specifically, is to help connect everyone in our organisation so they can support our customers. We like to remind our people that they are not just building software, they are helping our customers to serve those in need.

What I love about what I do is the opportunity to drive change and serve a bigger purpose. We are purpose led and connecting with humanity, not just providing insurtech solutions. It's about getting people to think about everything they do every day and understand how it impacts other people. That's the biggest driver for me; to get people to focus on that end goal. Yes, we still have to get these tasks done, but we are also transforming, changing and evolving. We support our people to consider what it might be like to step into the shoes of others. It's this duality of keeping the end goal in sight whilst also having the capacity to consider things from others' perspectives that drives us. When people tailor their understanding, they can see the result driving business results. I love seeing everyone in a position where they're bringing their very best selves to work, so they can best service our customers.

TELL US A LITTLE ABOUT HOW COVID IMPACTED WHAT YOU DO AND HOW YOU ADAPTED

FINEOS operates in multiple countries, so when COVID hit, the first thing for us was to make sure everyone was okay. 'And if you're not okay, here's your health support system.' That was the first thing we did – ensure everyone was aware that we (the leadership team) understood it was a stressful time and we wanted to make sure everyone was okay.

It was a practical approach in many ways; 'don't worry if you're at home with your kids or if your dog is in the background. We know it makes it hard to stay focused, do what you need to do – whatever you can do'. This was our standard in the early days of COVID. We also told our customers what we told our people, so expectations were managed. We set a standard and let them know that if they had any issues, they should come to the leadership team. We also made sure that everyone was set up so they knew exactly where to go to get their equipment and who to go to if they had any problems or needed support. Initially we set up daily communication in every country, saying 'this is what is happening in your country'. These moved to weekly as time progressed. We also set up other support systems for mental and physical wellbeing.

We had gym classes online, groups for those who wanted to walk and events for charity, like 'how many kilometres could we do?' We got people involved in those sorts of activities that kept up their interest and interaction. We essentially set up multiple employee interest groups. We had people doing different things, from reading books to cooking online. It's keeping people connected, engaged, and also empowered them to get their job done. They were still wanting to come to work for the social side as much as for the work. We also created similar initiatives with our global customers. We had to make sure that we were delivering, and this meant helping our customers deliver on their projects.

We were already operating in the digital world, so we had that advantage, but what did come to light were all the organisations, particularly who weren't cloud-based, realised quickly that this was the new era where users/employees needed to access technology remotely and securely. For many of them, it highlighted the importance of cloud-based technology and that they now had to move forward into the digital world. Working through COVID changed our business model, and it certainly changed the business model for many of our customers too in how we worked together. We all had to think differently. We asked ourselves, *What are the things we need to think about in the future?* because if we were doing this, we could help our customers do it too. Many realised they needed to lean into digitalisation and transformation, and that by not doing that, they were going to fall behind. There was real incentive and motive for rapid change.

Our core strategy was around keeping connected with our customers and our people. Our biggest focus for us, was internal, because we can have the best strategy and the best products, but unless you have your people fully engaged with their hearts and minds, no-one is going to win in the end. This meant allowing people to work when it suited them. Using technology was a massive factor in helping us engage with everyone. We had ways to engage socially and physically, not just operations, and we even had health care online if they needed to talk to someone. At the end of the day, it doesn't matter if you're a technology company or the end person, the human side will always be there.

Looking back, COVID has certainly accelerated change, particularly around the digital space, but it's also encouraged people to reassess what matters and how you connect. I think for many, they have discovered there are better things to be doing with their life, and they're actually enjoying the real things in life now.

What stands out for me, though, has been the change in resilience of our business and our people. It didn't happen overnight, but it has enabled us to weather the storm. For example, we had two mergers and acquisitions during this time – a massive change for any company in the best of times. On top of all of the COVID-related changes, we were bringing in another company with their own culture, people and customers and then … we did it again! But we were very secure and confident that we would be able to do that because we have such a strong culture.

As an organisation we're used to dealing in different time zones, with different cultures and with change. But what really drove this capacity was our ability to bring it back to our purpose and what we needed to do. To be honest, it doesn't matter about the environment outside of that. It's about bringing our best selves and doing what we could when we could.

TELL US ABOUT DEALING WITH CONFUSION, CHANGE AND CONFLICT SINCE WE'VE BEEN IMPACTED BY COVID

We did see a lot of change during these times, and even though we put a lot of things in place to talk to people, to share with them what was going on, we also recognised we had a lot of work to do with our leadership to support them too. We had to draw them in and do a modernised leadership program. During COVID, we invested heavily in our leadership teams so they truly understood the importance of clarity, alignment and engagement, specifically when people felt isolated or were struggling. This was a massive change for everyone, individually and for our organisation.

How did we change? We were already digital, we were already remote to some degree, so those things didn't change as much, but how we managed our people, how we led our people and how we worked to engage with our people – this was a massive change. We had a lot of work to do to make sure our internal compass, our foundational stone, was supported by the right tools and strategies. And just as important, we had to ensure our leaders were fully engaging with our teams and cross-communicating so that silos weren't created. We didn't want people to feel isolated or left alone to do their own thing. We put a lot of emphasis on that while having difficult conversations on performance or conflict when not face to face.

Some of the biggest challenges for us have been in the 'unlearning'. It's not learning the new stuff that's hard, but unlearning all the old stuff. I have a saying I picked up from a book I once read, 'Drop the Kylie!' It's in reference to the song 'Better the Devil You Know' by Kylie Minogue, implying that *the devil you know* isn't better, and in fact, we must 'drop this'. We make sure that people know change is constant and you must keep moving forward. 'What got us here, won't get us there' is one of our leadership principles. A lot of people are afraid to fail, and they're afraid of what that looks like, but when you look at the most successful people, they don't look at failure that way; they win or they learn. They take that learning, they're resilient, and they get back up and they do it again in a different way. For the people who don't do that, who are afraid or resist the change, they get stuck and end up in a downward spiral, because if you aren't moving forward, you are going backwards.

Ultimately, it comes down to the mindset you have about change. Even when dealing with conflict, think for five seconds only and step into their shoes for a second. You'll see it from a different perspective. That's what the essence of diversity and inclusion is all about. It's looking at different perspectives, different personalities, different ways of learning, different ways of thinking, and then working forward together.

For many, COVID was a time of isolation, we had people who were maybe sharing an apartment, or people who didn't have a workstation. There were people with a lot of young kids at home, trying to juggle homeschooling, their house and their work. We needed to make this as easy for them as possible. Which is why we said, 'Work times that works best for you,' or, 'Where can we help you set up a workspace?' We tried to keep connected with those people. When things started to loosen up, we also gave people choices. We went out of our way to ensure we asked everybody, 'How are you doing and what can we do to help?' Post-COVID, we've given people options: either going to the office, working from home or a little bit of both. It's all about making sure everyone is treated equally. I think, as a business, you must continuously keep up with that and make sure that you are addressing the diverse needs of everyone in your organisation to keep that motivation going and keep them engaged. Our retention rate is great because of that, and I put it down to that factor. *Because we hear people. We don't listen to respond, we listen to understand … and then we respond.*

TELL US ABOUT THE CRAICS, CROCODILE TEARS AND STANDOUT MOMENTS FROM THE LAST FEW YEARS

Reflecting on that moment when we were closing our office because of COVID, it was surreal. We had everyone out of the office and needed to them set up at home. We were in the boardroom, and I was there helping our IT team get equipment out and do things like that. It was a real *oh my goodness, what is going on in the world right now?* moment. What was going on? We all thought it was going to be two weeks. I was actually kind of excited. *This is going to be great; I get to work from home, no commute.* But as time went on, I think what was scary was not being able to see your friends or your family; my mum lives a four-hour drive away. After we got about two months in, I hadn't seen my family or friends, and I felt completely consumed by work. I was trying to help all our people and our customers, I felt that I had done all that, but I definitely hadn't considered myself. I hadn't even considered my own family. There was a moment where I was like, *Oh my God, this is real life, I'm trying to keep everyone up, but actually, I'm not looking after me.* It was an aha moment. But I also felt empathy for those who were doing it worse than me. This insight gave me an appreciation for being much more empathetic towards everyone's situation during COVID. It was such a conflicted time, because here I was voicing how busy I was at work and there were so many people who lost their jobs, struggling with mortgages. It made me grateful too but then the conflict was a sense of guilt for feeling that exhausted.

I think the high moments for me were when we were able to connect globally. It was such a wonderful thing to bring together people from across different nations, cultures and families. We did a few concerts but there was a special show we did in 2021;

we hosted a magic show online with Keith Barry. We got all our people, their kids, families and friends online at the same time. It was middle of the night for some people, but we just encouraged as many people as possible to join us. And we recorded it for those who couldn't join us live. It was amazing to see everyone's posts as we brought a sense of deeper connection into our community. It really broadened our company, as it wasn't just about work but about our people. And we built upon this. We did entertainment sessions where people would sing, play their guitar; we'd send gratitude journals to everyone; we did pizza nights where we sent families pizza and we all joined in. It was like a big, massive remote party. It was so special.

SHARE YOUR HACKS, INNOVATIONS OR LEARNINGS THAT HAVE EMERGED FROM THIS TIME

Change culture – what has really stood out for me has been the resilience of our business and of our people. This isn't by accident. We have worked hard to create a culture of change resilience, and navigating COVID has shown me how critical it has been to get our foundations right.

About ten years ago, our leadership team sat down, and we wrote and developed this thing called a 'playbook'. Even as we have evolved over time, our playbook has been a constant. It tells us about where we're going, our purpose, our mission and our values. This playbook informs our pillars across market, product, customers, people and financials. It enables us to cross-fertilise naturally though our goals. It has made it easier for people to step into the shoes of others and our people know they are dependent on each other. This has really set the tone for our company 'One-Team'. It has enabled us to constantly evolve.

Every quarter, we talk about our focus, what we want, what is working well and where we need to change. Our people understand from a holistic point of view, where we are going and if and why we need to change.

We have also supported this culture of change resilience through our change management playbook. This steps out what good process looks like and creates a safe and structured ecosystem. These intersections of playbooks help us provide a clear 'why' as well as giving our people a voice. They know they are heard and are part of the process. This is what ultimately enables us to create a culture and business model that is resilient and readily able to adapt and change.

We have made this real by making one of our 'aspirational' values to positively challenge and help people accept positive challenge. We try to weave this into a lot of our practices. This all reinforces a change mindset, why there is often a need to change the status quo, always evolve, accept change and understand that you're going to be challenged.

For us, it is making sure that everything we do in our communications or practices comes back to our core playbook of where we're going. These are our values, and this is how we behave. This is our strategy, and this is the part you play. With all this in play, we are going to evolve. That playbook is ten years old, but is very much the heart of our business, I call it the internal compass; it's our North Star and always guides us to where we're going.

What we really learned is that our playbook and our internal compass is keeping our heartbeat constant. It's what has kept us connected and will remain keeping us connected throughout the future, whatever that may bring.

LOOKING FORWARD, WHAT DO YOU THINK MIGHT BE SOME LASTING TRENDS OR INFLUENCES?

I think what's shaping the world for us is the digital transformation. It has impacted everyone. It's got us to think about the world outside and how the world is going forward. We're constantly thinking about our market and who we're serving, and what that looks like post-COVID. And from all the lessons we've learnt, I think looking forward is about making sure we continue to connect, and we continue to do that in a way that's also structured.

More and more organisations are waking to the importance of being purpose led, getting to the hearts and minds of people. When you're leading a company with a purpose to serve humanity, then everyone has a purpose to serve. This connects us across the organisation, and smart companies are catching on to this. It is a shift away from a prioritisation and focus on 'tech' or 'business profit' because when you win the hearts and minds of people, when you offer a great service or a great product, customers will come back. For us, it's enabling our people and focusing on what they need to do, using their skills, to be part of that overall ecosystem. The reality is that most people think, *I don't have time to do much charity work,* (I know that I don't) but actually, the work we are doing every day is helping a bigger cause and purpose. If you can get people to think that way, it drives the motivation to get out of bed in the morning.

What does the future look like for us? I think we will continue to expand. We'll continue to work globally, and I am really excited because I think as an organisation, we are much more open to responding to different needs. During COVID, one of our people said, 'I can't wait for my new organisation to see my new wheels.' We didn't know if that someone was in a wheelchair, we never knew, nor should we know, but if we were in an office, we would have noticed those things. So, it has brought a new level of awareness internally, we don't assume and we don't label. That has driven a bit of a change in our culture. Even with how we are thinking about our impact on the environment. We are considering if we really 'need' those offices or if we actually need to fly to these places. COVID has caused us to consider the impact to energy, environment, finances and our people, and I believe that will be a lasting trend for us.

Look at the world, we're in an environment that has also become a massive part of our culture. We are asking ourselves how do we reward and engage people to help drive that awareness? Are we thinking sustainably and is this right for our people? Although we're not manufacturing and we don't have a huge carbon footprint, we can definitely play our part. We can all help with understanding different cultures and needs and contribute to the conversation about creating sustainability as an organisation. The environment has probably been one of the big influences we're trying to drive now as a strategy, around sustainability, making sure we're doing things ethically. We're asking all our people who supply to us the same thing, to ensure we are all aligned with our culture and our purpose. Once we have that alignment within the whole ecosystem, I think we'll all do a better job, which is to help humankind. I don't care what kind of company you are, at the end of the day, that's what you should be thinking about.

YOUR TIPS FOR DEALING WITH PEOPLE DYNAMICS DURING CONFUSION, CHANGE AND CONFLICT

For people who are trying to bring about the change:
- Step in the shoes of the other person.
- It is really important and helps to cut through assumptions. Understand that not everyone is the same, be open to being challenged and take into consideration somebody's perspective, whether you agree with it or not.
- Listen to understand. And take it onboard. Listening to understand is important when you are trying to drive change. When we listen to understand it helps us identify our assumptions and bias. Listening to understanding is an active thing – acknowledge it and implement it in a mutually respectful way.
- Share the benefits. It's important to clearly communicate the benefits of why change is important. Even though you explain why you're doing something, when you tell people the benefits of the change it will help create the incentive for why they need to change. Don't assume they know or understand – be clear and consistent.

For the people who are in change, the change is happening for them, it's also difficult:
- Mindset shift. Hopefully through our experiences since COVID, we've come to realise that everything changes and how we are today has changed; the way the world 'is' has changed. There must be a mindset around accepting that change will happen. Just be open to understanding why the change is needed.
- Get clarity. If you aren't clear about why change might be needed or what the benefits are, then it's your responsibility to

ask the questions. If you don't have clarity about the positive benefits, then you need to create the dialogue and the conversation. Once you have clarity and you understand why, you can move forward and be part of the change.

- Choose your change. As the recipient of change, it's important to think about how you can impact change in a positive way, *What is the positive in this for me?* Sometimes the change isn't going to work for you, it may go against you, and as difficult as that is, it can be the reality, so you still need to make a choice.

BIO

As chief people officer, Joanne is responsible for leading global human resources, learning and development practices and change management programs across the organisation. Her goal is to deliver an employee-oriented, high-performance culture, aligned to support the organisational growth strategy. Joanne has held senior HR positions since joining FINEOS in 2000. She was responsible for expanding the HR team and introducing global HR support procedures to support eight new countries. Prior to joining FINEOS, Joanne held several leadership and key roles across various industries including recruitment, insurance and banking.

FINEOS is a global software company providing modern customer-centre core software to the employee benefits and life, accident and health industry. They help their customers move on from outdated legacy administration systems to our modern, purpose-built, customer-centric core product-suit. FINEOS recently received the 2022 Business & Finance Elevation Award and 2022 Technology Ireland Digital Technology Services Project of the Year awards to cap off a huge couple of years.

FINEOS.com
linkedin.com/in/joannemcmullan
linkedin.com/company/fineos/mycompany
twitter.com/fineos?s=11&t=ubUDO2mW-gxaNe7R8oaopg

LAURENCE BOULLE
DISLOCATING TIME REIMAGINING SPACE

We must also ask ourselves, Where will the more humanistic dimensions of dispute resolution end up in this increasing on-line environment?

Unfortunately, we often measure what is easy to measure, and don't measure what is sometimes important to measure.

TELL US ABOUT WHAT YOU DO AND WHAT YOU LOVE ABOUT WHAT YOU DO

As a dispute resolver for about three decades now, after five years in legal practice and an academic involved in writing and policy-making in various areas, one of my early observations was how COVID and the lockdowns distorted both space and time. I think there was an initial moment of reflection, with everyone initially thinking *What next?* but it didn't take long to test the tolerance of uncertainty. As we know, humans want to be certain, even if we're wrong, and it's hard to say how long it took, but it wasn't too long before a new kind of familiarity was built into the dispute resolution systems forced upon us.

For me, personally, I was physically dislocated from where I do most of my mediations, which are in Sydney, as I had moved just days before lockdown. And in a sense, the justice system did pause for a moment; the High Court, of course, stopped operating altogether. But with mediations and arbitrations there was only a short lull, before things began to pick up again.

Of course, interactions with fellow mediators and co-workers changed. There were some relationships that were reinforced, but I felt a real loss of not going into the Personal Injury Commission in Sydney, where I would regularly meet people I'd known, in some cases, for twenty years. I missed the familiar family feel about it, the small talk and interesting discussions. I had been feeling a bit deprived in that department, so I recently decided to go to the Resolution Institute conference, held in Sydney in October 2022, and it was it was great fun; getting that sense of familiarity and collegiality back again, in person, as opposed to a virtual environment.

From my observations about the work we do, I like it when

it's effective. I feel we are in a world where so many professional services have become undervalued. But I still believe there is a kind of residual value for bringing, as they say, a literal 'peace' into the room. Even if that may be minimal sometimes, as in just getting a commercial settlement for a dollar value, while at other times it's more substantial, where there's a deeper sense of resolution. Though, I don't think this was overly impacted by COVID.

Certainly, at the beginning of the pandemic, we all had to adapt to the dislocation of time, in a sense that we often see 'time' as a sort of linear arrow, you know, racing towards us and then disappearing, going straight through to an unknown destination. Early on, at least, there seemed to be a more kind of cyclical sense of time, which touches traditional cultures and has a close link with space. If we go back in time all forms of dispute resolution or dispute determinations, like courts, arbitration and reconciliation, were identified historically with a certain space-time, if you like. For me, for the first time, it felt like there was a complete dislocation between the two. I appreciate, that as much as fifteen years ago, I was doing things partly online, through video-conferencing and telephone, but suddenly, this was a far bigger dislocation, and space, and its time connection, felt very different. People were now in their homes, with dogs, birdsong and children. We were able to shift between synchronous and asynchronous time and feel comfortable doing it, and still are now. It's not exclusive to pandemic or lockdown situations, but it was certainly accentuated.

TELL US A LITTLE ABOUT HOW COVID IMPACTED WHAT YOU DO AND HOW YOU ADAPTED

Interestingly, I've tended over the years to move from one conflict area to another, for example from community to family to native title. At the moment, I mainly work in two broad areas; one is common law work injury cases, and the other is small business, which can sometimes be 'quite big' business. However, the one area in which there was a big change, and probably many people may have experienced this, is in relation to impacted lessees, both commercial and retail. Under the national code and state regulations, there was an obligation for lessors and lessees to negotiate. And then to come to something called 'binding mediation', as was stipulated. This didn't mean that the mediator made a binding decision, but that the mediated outcome would be binding, so that was an interesting kind of new area of practice. And I'm sure there were many others induced by the pandemic.

But in terms of the more attitudinal aspects, I guess I was struck in the beginning with a change of habits towards a kinder generosity of spirit and acceptance that, as we know, technology doesn't always work. There was also a new sense of time, to some extent, or at least in my perception of it. But I don't think that lasted the whole of lockdown. I think I've seen some of the old habits return.

Initially, though, it was a time when you'd have long telephone conversations with people, I mean social ones, instead of the much more peremptory kind of conversation we'd been used to. I thought there was a lean towards a warmer human spirit, a kinder, helping-hand approach.

I found using the old technique of mediator vulnerability was easier online than in face-to-face meetings. Being able to be more open to human vulnerability in terms of the technology, time constraints and switching to break-out rooms was interesting. As well as having to be more 'theatrical', as in when reading a document holding it up to the camera, so everyone knows what you're reading.

Another interesting element was that the dynamics between principal and agent, say an the injured worker or small business owner and their representatives, changed slightly. In the online environment, no longer could the lawyer, both physically and metaphorically, 'stand in front' of their client. All of sudden, agents and principals were more equal, both being the size of a postage stamp on-screen. It was less easy for a powerful barrister to dominate the space and the airtime.

In one matter we were three and a half hours into a commercial case, and things were becoming sticky! One of the clients asked, 'Can I speak to the client on the other side, separately?' I ran it past the advisers, and after the client breakout session, participation in the process became a little more egalitarian, a little more democratic, if you like.

TELL US ABOUT DEALING WITH CONFUSION, CHANGE AND CONFLICT SINCE WE'VE BEEN IMPACTED BY COVID

Interesting that the stories that always stick in my mind are the negatives or accounts of a disaster!

There are a lot of inevitable stories with technology not working. I had an overseas client, somewhere in North America, who was having difficulty on the platform they were using. Eventually, the compromise was that they would phone in – though it was still not a particularly good line. I then put them on speakerphone on my mobile phone so others could hear and respond.

There was more disjunction than I'd expected in terms of how people could participate. It was a challenge of adaption and fitting the forum to the fuss, as the old saying goes.

Another issue, which I'm sure others have experienced, was when there were people in a room but not in front of the camera. I learnt to always indicate beforehand that I wanted to know and see everybody who was in the room, at least in the open sessions, though it wouldn't apply in break-out sessions in which parties could confer with whoever they wanted. Several people were reluctant to be in front of the camera, either through ignorance or being fearful of contributing ... or perhaps they were still in pyjamas.

I also experienced a level of awkwardness at the beginning of meetings as participants would come online in a staggered process, so I'd be admitting people into joint sessions, and someone would be delayed, usually for good reason, but we couldn't start the meeting without them, so there'd be a period of small talk ... or not! They were difficult moments ... what do we talk about? I'm not that good with pleasantries and chatter, but some barristers are brilliant at greasing the parts. Otherwise we would be looking at each other with fixed stares or avoiding eye contact. Uncomfortable moments!

I sometimes feel like an accidental tourist in this whole dispute resolution thing, because we don't have control over many situations. You've got two or four or eight people, each playing a big part. There is a degree of professional satisfaction when things go well and I enjoy being a mediator in most cases. But sometimes I take work home, and continue 'mediating', and losing face because of it – I've had my kids on many occasions telling me, 'Don't mediate me!'

SHARE YOUR HACKS, INNOVATIONS OR LEARNINGS THAT HAVE EMERGED FROM THIS TIME

For the first time in my life, I became a 'trained actor', exposing me to some innovative learning that I'd never experienced before. One of the agencies I work for got all the dispute resolvers to do an excellent session on performing on screen, run by NIDA (National Institute of Dramatic Art). The young actors taught tips and tricks that I recognised we'd being doing in a small way for some years. They taught us to prepare ahead of sessions by stretching the body, doing breathing exercises and undertaking ugly chewing simulations, to be well lubricated for what was ahead. This touched on a thought I've been having for some time about bodily cognition and how it affects the brain and decision-making. We often forget what's going on physically and how the neural pathways can reflect the physiology of the body. Or conversely, how our powerful cognitive capacities can filter physiological formation.

I found the lessons helpful, not only in terms of preparation for online dispute resolution, but also for performance during online sessions: slightly exaggerating tone, pitch and prosody to be understood better on-screen. Because as I've mentioned before, when you're on-screen, your appearance is sometimes no larger in size than a postage stamp! Talking with slightly exaggerated movements can have a massive effect on comprehension and engagement online. This course was really my initiation into COVID-based dispute resolution, providing a greater understanding of what it's like to appear on-screen and what sort of contribution theatrics can make.

The thing I leaned into to the greatest extent during lockdowns was my use of 'screenshare'. Over time, I developed a whole set of documents, cartoons, photographs, charts, quotations and the like that I could keep in my figurative toolbox and use when appropriate. I have a couple of favourite cartoons that seem to 'lighten up' people's attitude: one is of two people building an old-fashioned bridge with stones, and the other is more accusatory, with pointing fingers. Each provides a useful metaphor for mediation use. I've been able to screen-share quotes from judges on the realities of litigation, which in face-to-face situations would involve physical handouts. I recycle the documents and images regularly. They stimulate both sides of the brain, making participants become a little less left-brain dominant. If things got to a certain level of discussion, I'd pull up a cartoon. I feel this is a facility which can't as easily be matched offline. Even just in having the names of the participants easily seen, in developing agendas, in using negotiation schedules for linked bargaining and in joint drafting of settlements or deeds, I found use of screenshare to be efficient and effective.

In fact, I have been thinking of running a seminar, online, entitled *Back Offline,* covering all the things we learnt during forced virtual mediation and considering what we can gain from it in the offline environment. In the case of document sharing, access spreadsheets and even using virtual whiteboards I don't think we can quite measure up in the offline environment to what we've achieved online in the last couple of years.

LOOKING FORWARD, WHAT DO YOU THINK MIGHT BE SOME LASTING TRENDS OR INFLUENCES?

Looking at forward trends coming out of COVID, as a person passionate about caring for the planet, I feel I should mention the environment and the question of whether what we're doing with a high dependency on electronics and technology is consumer and climate friendly. A book I read recently by Toby Walsh, *Machines Behaving Badly*, addresses this issue in depth, and it's been found that in regard to energy consumption, where we are now is much better than the old normal, with two exceptions – cryptocurrency and blockchain, which are highly energy dependent. While emails, websites and other online facilities are not carbon free, they generally involve fewer emissions than offline forms of dispute resolution.

The world did stop and pause for a moment during the pandemic, but there seems to be a mad rush for us to 'get back to normal'. We are all just creatures of habit, after all. But just because something is 'normal', doesn't automatically mean it is 'good'.

More generally, I think we've moved way beyond the notion of 'in-person' versus 'online'. It really has to be a mix of both worlds. Even in the online environment, I'm sure most dispute resolvers were still using a mix of mediums. There would be emails and text messages going on during the online meetings, and I was actually encouraging all of that. I thought all those supplementary methods were terrific, even if it was just a text message from counsel saying, *Slow but steady progress*. The notion of negotiation and mediation involving exclusively one form of communication is probably outdated.

Moving forward, I expect that when we're online, with all these facilities at our fingertips, we will be much more open to artificial intelligence in dispute resolution. The ability to bring in, say, predictive analytics into well-worn paths, whether it's matrimonial property or leasing outcomes, will be in a form that's easily manipulated in the moment. Big data management is another areas in which the algorithms will be useful. I suspect these and many other factors will play out more extensively in the future.

But I suppose the reservation goes to the initial point I made about how time and space have become so elastic in this environment. They're just not what we thought they were. Reflecting on that, I'd like to mention Tyson Yunkaporta, from Deakin University, and his book, *Sand Talk*.

Aboriginal epistemology is very much based around traditional conceptions of 'country', and if we go predominantly online, we may end up dislocating that whole concept of customary knowledge. In a recent climate change case, traditional owners objected to a large gas project and the technical issue in question was whether the Munupi people had been properly consulted, as required by legislation. Of significance in the case is that Justice Bromberg allowed evidence to be taken on Melville Island in the Torres Strait Islands, the objectors' country. This provided a real physicality to the evidence, a kind of walking and talking the territory, so to speak. Not only that, but evidence was given through words, dance and song. Through these presentations the court heard that the Munupi people feared that the development would damage the environment, including the ocean and shores, and impact on their way of life and spiritual wellbeing.

The value propositions considered by the court are exactly those that can be dealt with in dispute resolution processes. The judgement provides both encouragement and security for dispute resolvers in this regard. However, the narrative highlights the importance of country, epistemology and ways of communicating in traditional culture – which should not be allowed to disappear by over-digitalising everything.

Another factor, which is both positive and negative, is that if we are dispute resolving online it will be easier for measurement metrics to come into place. The masters of the universe will know exactly when we started and finished, how long it took, how much it cost and how long the breaks were. Unfortunately, we often measure what is easy to measure and don't measure what is sometimes *important* to measure. So, I think in the future, we might shift towards the quantitative efficiency notion of measurement which is only a partial indicator of effectiveness. Moreover, when one is online, everything is logged and recorded to some degree, and that could have impacts on privacy and confidentiality.

We must also ask ourselves, *Where will the more humanistic dimensions of dispute resolution end up in this environment?* There are people with disabilities, for example, in not being able to manage a keyboard. For such people there is still an important place for offline interaction.

YOUR TIPS FOR DEALING WITH PEOPLE DYNAMICS DURING CONFUSION, CHANGE AND CONFLICT

I still think the most profound tips are those things we learned way back when we began our careers as dispute resolvers. These tips are conventiona, but for me, were reinforced during the pandemic.

- To acknowledge. Although I think this is a bit more difficult in the online environment, acknowledging clients and advisers alike is really important. It's not just about listening. This factor is nothing new, but I think we must make the extra effort to be 'good acknowledgers'.
- To be patient. At the beginning of the pandemic this was a lot easier as there seemed to be more generosity of spirit in dispute resolution setting. I feel, however, that patience is an

imperative in our environments, despite money driving most things.
- To be persistent. Again, this is not new in dispute resolution and we are in a different environment post-COVID, but what can sometimes seem an impossible mission is never necessarily hopeless. Here we can draw on our experience, and with persistence, move to potential outcomes.

BIO

Laurence Boulle has been Belle Wiese of Legal Ethics (fractional) at the Newcastle Law School since 2017. He teaches mainly the commercial dispute resolution subject to both undergraduate and graduate students. Laurence coached the Newcastle team at the International Chamber of Commerce Mediation Competition in early 2019 and in December 2018 was co-supervisor of the student study tour to Cambodia. Based in Sydney and the Gold Coast, he has held senior appointments at three Australian universities and has taught at four others. He has been visiting professor at Gent University in Belgium, the University of Cape Town in South Africa and the University of the South Pacific in Vanuatu and Fiji.

After several years in legal practice, Laurence became an academic and shortly thereafter established a mediation practice. For nearly thirty years he has mediated a wide variety of disputes in different states and territories, and abroad: community, family, native title, general commercial, workers' compensation, personal injury, intellectual property, workplace and organisational. He has conducted dispute resolution workshops and seminars in all states and territories and in twelve overseas countries – from the Cook Islands to Sweden. Laurence's latest book is with Rachael Field, *Mediation in Australia* (LexisNexis, Sydney, 2018). He has written, co-authored or edited over twenty other books on mediation, constitutional law, globalisation, employment law and mediation. His books have been published in seven countries.

MEGAN MACNEILL
ACCELERATED LEARNING

You can't let fear be the reason you don't show up.

Organisations want to have some control over what their people are posting about and what they can and can't say. Now, I'm all for putting a policy in place because you don't want any bad language or anything that's derogatory, but you also can't strip away someone's personality, because that's the whole point of social media.

TELL US ABOUT WHAT YOU DO AND WHAT YOU LOVE ABOUT WHAT YOU DO

I'm a performance partner and personal brand strategist for business leaders. I assist business owners who have gone out on their own, starting very small, to now running a sizable company. They now have a significant turnover, staff and other responsibilities they never had before. And with that comes a lot of friction, because even if you wanted to put twenty-four hours a day into your business, obviously you can't. Often, you feel it's much easier to do it yourself. There are trust issues as your business grows with other people involved. Your passion for why you started is still there, but it is buried under the new responsibilities that come with success; that's where I come in.

Firstly, we look at how you are preforming right now with a 360 audit. Then we look at what legacy you want to leave and be remembered by, how long you are planning to be in the business and whether you can put systems in place so the business operates organically. It's about how your performance and personal brand are aligned and connecting you with your goals for you and your business. And of course, there is a lot of mind work involved. There is a lot to unpack; you'd be surprised how vulnerable my clients are during sessions and the strength it gives them. It is probably my favourite part.

My background is in psychology and branding from university, and I tend to lean into my knowledge in that area, because it doesn't matter whether you are selling a service or a product, people buy from people. It's not about flashy marketing campaigns or being on a billboard, it's way more than that, and I'm passionate about how psychology influences performance.

TELL US A LITTLE ABOUT HOW COVID IMPACTED WHAT YOU DO AND HOW YOU ADAPTED

I was CEO of a small not-for-profit business, The Rural Regional and Remote Women's Network. I absolutely loved it and am very passionate about the regions because it's where I started when I first immigrated to Australia and I'd made a lot of connections out in rural and regional WA. I am also a passionate advocate for gender equity so it was a fantastic role for me, combining multiple interests and passions, but I wanted to run my own business. I had already started making some headway into my own venture, so I decided, at the end of 2019, to let them know I would be leaving in April of 2020. And then, of course, in March, COVID came along. I had obviously handed in my notice and helped to get the next person onboard, so suddenly I had no job in an uncertain environment. My business wasn't quite up and running, and I thought, *Never mind – let's just go for it.* So, in the middle of lockdown, I went headfirst into business. At that point, it was very personal branding focused, nothing else. And to be honest, I wasn't happy with the terminology 'personal branding', which I still think a lot of people mostly relate to social media and getting 'likes'. What personal branding really is, is what people think, feel and say about you, but trying to translate that to my target audience isn't always easy. When COVID came along everybody was stuck behind a computer, and suddenly, there were no networking events and no chance of bumping into people on the terrace, and they were starting to wonder, *What if I am forgotten about?* That's when people started thinking, *Ah, Megan was onto something there.*

If the people that you need to notice you aren't seeing or hearing from you, essentially you don't exist and those who are showing up get the opportunities. This goes for potential clients, job offers, speaking opportunities, attracting staff – absolutely anyone that you need in order to have the impact you want.

So, COVID was terrible for me in one way, because I wasn't prepared for starting a business in those conditions, but it was great in another way, because people started to think more seriously about how they were positioned and what was going to take them to the next level coming out of COVID, or even how they were going to survive it.

In a way, COVID accelerated people to think about how they connect with the people and the world around them. When you think about your brand, it can be as simple as how you are looking after your team. All of my clients had to go into lockdown, and it looked different for each of them. Some were still able to go into the office because of the type of work that they did. While some businesses shut down; there were a whole variety of things happening. I noticed that the ones who did the best during COVID, and are still doing the best now, are the ones who had good communication throughout. They were the leaders with the strongest personal brands because their staff knew exactly what they could and couldn't go to them for. They still had an open-door policy, even though they were in different locations. Generally, in an office, leaders can decide to have either an open-door policy or a closed-door policy. Open-door allows co-workers to come in and discuss issues, which means that your day might be longer. But how would you translate that when you're not in the same room or the same building? That was really interesting the way different leaders responded. Well, which ones were leading, and which ones were managing.

It always comes back to personal brand and leadership. And it's not just about keeping staff engaged through and post-COVID, but externally as well, in terms of getting new clients, or current clients having confidence in you as a leader. A big factor was how information was being shared and who was putting out that information, who was actually calling clients and staff to keep them updated and who was letting everyone know relevant updated legislation.

With the clients I worked closely with, we were working heavily on that communication, in terms of newsletters and making sure everyone knew about new legislation coming out, what you had access to funding-wise, what you were and weren't allowed to do and how business could actually operate now. Trusted leaders were distilling that information, almost playing the role of journalists, really, getting all the high-level information and breaking it down so their teams didn't have to ask, 'What is going on, and what the hell does this mean for me?' And they were distilling it down in a way that said, 'Okay, don't worry about this. We've read all this for you and we're communicating it back in a language you can understand.' The leaders that did it really well, were not only talking to their staff and clients, but to a wider audience as well, which then attracted new clients. I heard a lot of people say, 'COVID was horrendous, I couldn't get new clients and couldn't do anything,' but I disagree. If you played the role of helper, saviour or journalist in your field, you were their trusted figure in a time of real uncertainty.

In Western Australia, we were relatively lucky in terms of lockdowns, and I saw some clients who never prepared for it as they didn't think it was going to last very long. They didn't even improve their technology or change their processes at all. They're still doing things the way they've always been done. And that's working for them okay for now, but will it in the future? Whereas there were others who completely adapted. With a snap of the fingers, they now have hybrid working environments. Even when the lockdowns were over, they didn't make it mandatory to be working back in the office, they kept things working in a hybrid way, even before it was cool to start talking about hybrid workplaces. This was happening early on in WA, as we didn't have many COVID cases, whereas the rest of the world is only catching up with hybrid environments now. There was probably a missed opportunity, I think, for Western Australia as a whole, to be the testing ground for what hybrid working could look like, as I feel most places went back to 'business as usual'. But I have seen some really great examples of people who implemented that very early on and were way ahead of the curve. And they've managed to maintain the staff numbers they had prior to COVID, because their team knows that when anything happens, these leaders have got their back. They're looking after them. They weren't just managing their team, they were leading their teams. That's leadership performance working, as well as strong personal branding building in action.

One of the ways I adapted during COVID was to set up some online networking events, to keep myself connected. A by-product was it strengthened my personal brand in that area too.

My parents gave me a bracelet when I was younger, with a little butterfly that said, *Social butterfly*. And I remember thinking, *I don't even like butterflies, I don't understand why you've given me this*. I didn't know what a social butterfly was, and it wasn't until I was a bit older that I realised what it meant. It's because I attract people, I gather great people and bring them together. When I was employed in a role, I had a title of CEO or marketing manager and I was invited to lots of events, because they wanted me at the table, I had a title they valued. When I started my own business, I had no value to anyone anymore. I was looking for business. And I thought, *Unless I do something to keep my network growing and my current network strong, I'm just going to disappear.* So, when COVID happened and I couldn't get to networking events whether I was invited or not, I started an online event every Wednesday at lunchtime, and if you wanted to, you could just jump on. We did a round table of what everyone was up to, which was different for everyone. Some people were still in the office, some people had to work from home, some had started businesses. Essentially, we were all in the same storm in different boats, but it was really good because everybody was able to brainstorm and help one another. We didn't get too personal in the main group, but then we went into little groups and paired off with another person. I called it Zoom roulette and often you'd pair off up to three times during the session, so you always got to meet someone new. But once things eased here in Western Australia, we had these events in real life, and it was brilliant, as we had quite a few misconceptions from what we'd perceived online, like, 'I thought you were taller.' We don't do that group anymore, but the great thing is the relationships have lasted and the collaborations that happened, and still do through that group, are phenomenal.

What's clear for me is the importance of investing in relationships. I think people are already worrying about AI and whether their job may not exist in the future, but if you're people focused, your job won't ever go. You might have some AI to assist you, but if you are working with people, you're not going to disappear. A robot can't do personal branding for you. You're either a good person or you're not a good person. You're either someone I like or you're not. A robot will not be able to fix that. A doctor may use a lot of AI to be able to diagnose patients, for example, but we are all still going to want that human touch. Yes, everyone's jobs will change, but there's still room for us, because we're all people working for people.

TELL US ABOUT DEALING WITH CONFUSION, CHANGE AND CONFLICT SINCE WE'VE BEEN IMPACTED BY COVID

How we communicate has definitely changed. Particularly because we have different generations in the workforce. Generally speaking, and this is very general, those who are leading at the moment, the CEOs and the decision-makers around town, might use something like LinkedIn and probably have Facebook for friends and family, but they weren't creating profiles on Instagram, so we didn't really get to know who they were. We would use LinkedIn to be able to have a glimpse into them, but what goes on LinkedIn is very much business based, so we weren't getting much of their personality. But all of a sudden, they found themselves at home. They didn't have an assistant and they weren't going to events. They didn't have someone creating content for them. Now they're at home saying, 'Working in the office with my dog and I can't believe how much I'm getting done.' Or, 'I can't believe how hard it is for women in the workplace. I'm now working at home with three kids here, and I never imagined what the balance would be or what the conflict for a woman in my position would be.' So, I think there was a change in perspective for a lot of leaders, as to what a work environment needs to look like. Also, more trust was probably gained, if it was done right, with the next generation coming behind them, because all of a sudden, they had empathy for them. Some snapped back to business as usual as soon as they could, while others have really stuck with it. And it's changed their whole business process. It's really important for the next generation of leaders to learn from this, as now we expect our leaders to have some sort of understanding of what each individual needs. And we also have some understanding now, lower down looking up, that they can't possibly understand *all of our needs*. So yes, I think there's been a shift in communication.

There has also been a big shift in the types of conflicts leaders have to deal with. Some of them have adapted quickly, depending on the work environment, with some environments having stringent rules around them. I'm quite lucky in that only one of my clients has an office globally, the rest are all local businesses. But friends who were working in national corporations were having to adapt to rules put in place by the east coast or overseas. The eastern states had a completely different experience with COVID than we did, so those rules were sometimes a bit silly in many ways. Whereas I've seen the clients I've worked with here, at least, being able to adapt to what WA needed.

One of the biggest areas of conflict has been around working online and with social media. Organisations want to have some control over what their people are posting about, and what they can and can't say. Now I'm all for putting a policy in place because you don't want any bad language or anything that's derogatory, but you also can't strip away someone's personality, because that's the whole point of social media. As a leader, you can leverage your staff brilliantly if you can get them online, because, if you've got great staff making digital footprints, yes they might eventually leave you, but it doesn't matter, because you have to concentrate on what value they're bringing right now. You've got to give them a little bit of freedom, and that can be hard because it's an unknown. So imagine when you have a new employee and you've sent them out to a networking event, generally speaking, someone from the office will go with them for the first couple of events, because you want to see what they are they like with other people – whether they drink too much when there's a free bar. Do they say silly things? Do they get into a nasty political debate with your best client? These are valid concerns. But when you're putting someone online and you're saying, 'Okay, I'd love you to be posting about the business and your experience here on your LinkedIn account, but I also want to hold your hand on that and vet what you say,' that's sending a conflicting message. Do you trust me or don't you?

It's important to understand the value of our personal brand when looking to upgrade our employment, because how many times have you seen someone who isn't as good as you get a job or an opportunity or a speaking gig that you think would suit you better? You may be technically better, but the difference is that person put their hand up, they had their head above the water, they had a stronger brand. When you're starting out in your first few jobs, it's fairly easy at entry level to get those first steps in, but as the jobs get fewer and fewer and as you go higher up, you can't just lean on what grades you got, and how you're performing on paper. You need to be instantly recognisable for the role or opportunity coming up. You want people to vouch for you and think of you before anyone else. That's why social proof is massive, and why we all want referrals. What other people say about us is so powerful. That's your personal brand.

It is changing and we can thank COVID. It accelerated it. This has always been happening. It used to be, 'Bob's uncle at the pub said …' but now it's, 'Someone on LinkedIn said …' We're now taking that digital word of mouth as seriously as we were taking in-person word of mouth. And that can also create conflict out in the world, because you have a lot of people who are sitting there saying, 'But I would have been better for that,' and the only answer to that is, 'You didn't show up.' You didn't keep showing up. You weren't remembered. You weren't top of mind at that given time. Which is totally okay, because we're not Kardashians, and we don't need to have the whole world know who we are. You've got to focus on the group of people who do need to know. You can't get every opportunity. There is enough work for everyone, but it does create conflict when you start seeing people in your field getting opportunities you would like. The Internet is great for showing you opportunities, but it's also great for showing you what you missed out on as well. You've got to ground yourself. It was going to happen anyway, but COVID maybe accelerated it.

TELL US ABOUT THE CRAICS, CROCODILE TEARS AND STANDOUT MOMENTS FROM THE LAST FEW YEARS

Probably the biggest for me is that I got engaged in 2019 and was meant to be going home to get married in April of 2020. In March, my wedding got postponed (and you may remember I'd also quit my job), and we thought it would just be postponed to the following year. It became apparent very quickly that it would have to be cancelled. But we were okay with that. We got married in a registry office, and we're happy. We've now got a baby; life is good. But the heartbreaking part was the fact that I couldn't see my parents at all. They couldn't get here, and I couldn't go home. The conflict wasn't the fact that I couldn't see them, because thanks to social media, I could speak to them every single day and video with them. But that will never replace seeing your family in real life. The conflict was really the comments that were made online where people wanted to keep the borders shut. And while I agreed with it to a certain extent, from a health and safety point of view, I think we kept them closed too long and I thought it was a bit stringent in the way they were doing it. You know, even citizens couldn't get home, which was really hard. But the comments around people like me who are not born and bred in Australia were harsh. 'You chose to be here.' 'You left your family.' 'Go home if you want to.' It was upsetting. I mean, I have a business, I bought a house, I'm married. My life is here. I've been here for ten years. I didn't leave my home with the intention of never being able to get back there again. I always have enough money in the bank, so that if I need to leave tomorrow, I can be home within twenty-four hours. That's always been my contingency plan. I've paid my taxes, and I'm just as much a part of this society as anyone. Some of the comments were horrible. Disgusting, in fact. This is my home, but it didn't feel like it anymore. People weren't understanding. I used to reply to a lot of misinformed comments on Facebook, which is a rabbit hole you shouldn't go down at three o'clock in the morning when you are upset because you haven't seen your parents for eighteen months. Personally, it was not a nice time for me.

It's shocking the level of hostility on social media, with very little justification for it. I learnt that people can be horrendous, and it's very important to surround yourself with the right people.

I use it all my time in my workshops that, 'You are the sum of the five people you spend the most time with.' ~ Jim Rohn.

It's so true, because you bounce off your energy from them. What happened, in this case, was that I was going down a rabbit hole of negative information. And this was not people that I would have ever socialised with or done business with. These were nobodies on the Internet with very negative opinions. They were small-minded and probably had never even travelled out of the state, and luckily for them everyone they loved was locked in the state with them. It was a reminder of how important your network is. The biggest learning is to remember who the important people are in your life, the VIPs, and to not dilute it down with the opinions of people that don't matter. When I first start working with my clients, I have them do a 360 audit on themselves, asking their family and associates things like, 'If you could describe me, what are some words you would use?' and, 'What is it you think I do?' Those sorts of general questions. And I'm always very adamant they don't send it to anyone whose opinion the don't value.

So I didn't really take my own advice in that time, and took things very personally, like people were telling me to 'go home!' I had to pinch myself and say, 'Why am I listening to the opinions of these people, because they're not my people!'

I don't know that I'm doing anything differently now because the whole situation resolved itself. Mum and Dad are here, it's one of those happy endings. What breaks my heart is the amount of people who didn't get to see their family for different reasons or because they passed away. I feel very grateful for the situation I'm in. I guess now I just don't take anything for granted. I take every opportunity I can to be with my family and the people that matter to me.

COVID is nothing in the scheme of things when there are wars and other global events taking place. But it does give you a perspective of what really matters. I think, subconsciously, I'm doing lots of things differently.

I have clients who are from overseas too and I know they also struggled. There was a lot of guilt as we sat here comfortably in our bubble while friends and family were battling health issues and job losses.

There were such complex perspectives and experiences for us

here in Western Australia, because of the really unique way that we were impacted by COVID, particularly compared to overseas. I caught up with a friend from America and she'd been watching a movie where people were in a public space without masks on, and it made her really anxious. She was wondering why they weren't wearing masks. I thought it was a little weird for her to say that, but then that was her world. Whereas our world wasn't like that.

One of the funny things that happened was when we got married at the registry office, in the middle of lockdown. We were only allowed five people in there. The five people were me and my husband, each of our witnesses and the registrar. I had asked my husband's sister to bring along our niece who was only eighteen months old, not really thinking that she would count in the limit restrictions. So, when we all arrived, the lady was like, 'There's only five allowed, she can't come in.' She was only eighteen months old, so she couldn't stay outside by herself, and I just couldn't quite get it into my head that a little human was counted as one of the five. That became quite a comical situation, where at one point, I thought I wouldn't be getting married that day. But her dad came to pick her up and we did get married. I had no idea you can get married in fifteen minutes, so I don't know why we have full-day events for these things. I have to tell myself that or I get upset I missed out on the big shindig!

SHARE YOUR HACKS, INNOVATIONS OR LEARNINGS THAT HAVE EMERGED FROM THIS TIME

You can't let fear be the reason you don't show up. We fear public speaking more than death. Like, that is an actual statistic! But that isn't your only option. You've got podcasts, social media, blogs, videos, writing books and so many other ways to communicate your message.

Pre-2019 how many people knew what Zoom was, let alone knew how to use it? Now we are all experts.

There is so much technology available to us. It is quick, easy and cheap to fail and get back up and try something else. So try it.

Find out the target audiences that you need to be in front of and remember you're not a Kardashian. You don't need to get a million views on your Instagram post. It's not about that. It's about a small target audience of the right people rather than the whole world. But then understanding that you have got the whole world at your fingertips. COVID was brilliant for saying you don't have to think small in your local market. If you can do something on your computer at home, or you can do it on a park bench somewhere, then you have access to a global market. You don't have to think small anymore. You can think as big as you like.

The gig economy was already becoming quite big before COVID. COVID just went, 'Hello, come on, Mr Gig Economy. This is your time.' A lot of people might think of that as cheap labour, sending stuff off overseas to get some graphics done, or your bookkeeping doing data entry, but no; it's for absolutely everything. Yes, there are some jobs that can be outsourced cheaply, but there's also a lot that needs to be of high quality, and people want to pay for high quality. You now have a global audience. You have the whole world at your doorstep. We may not have been able to get on planes, but as long as you had an internet connection, you could be anywhere.

LOOKING FORWARD, WHAT DO YOU THINK MIGHT BE SOME LASTING TRENDS OR INFLUENCES?

That it's people first, company second. Whether you're on TikTok, LinkedIn, Instagram, you name your platform, there's always new ones that are being developed. We've come back from companies trying to make themselves look massive, to companies trying to show who the individuals are within their organisation. It used to be that you'd phone a help desk for a big company and be waiting on the line for hours. These days, a quick Tweet, and suddenly, you're heard. These platforms are brilliant, allowing each and every single one of us to have a voice. And that's really powerful. But it's how you use that voice that's important. Choose your platform, choose your message, and it can take you absolutely anywhere. If you dilute it down, then it's just the same as being in-person and nothing has changed, but as long as you put out something coherent and you've got strategy behind it, the world is your oyster.

People have been upscaling more than ever and this will continue, particularly as we move forward into the technology of Web3. At the moment, Facebook owns absolutely everything. Everything you have on Facebook, Instagram and WhatsApp is owned by them, it's their platform and they're monetising it. Whereas with Web3, it's going to be owned by the individual. You are a content creator and you're the one that owns it. You're the one that's going to benefit from it. It's going to grow you and your business. Whereas now, we're all using platforms that are free to us, but we don't own it, someone else does. You're putting your stuff out there, but someone else has ownership of it. Twisting that around is going to change things. Did COVID accelerate that? Maybe. I don't think there'll be a person in the country, or possibly the world, who has a computer and hasn't upskilled their tech skills. People can use the technology better, which means as more is added, it's familiar to them. So that has sped things up.

Web3 is going to be the next game changer. That's nothing to do with COVID but that might need a whole other book!

YOUR TIPS FOR DEALING WITH PEOPLE DYNAMICS DURING CONFUSION, CHANGE AND CONFLICT

- Whatever situation is causing conflict, try putting yourself in the other person's shoes every time. You must try and think the way they're thinking. There are three different communication styles. There are people who think, people who feel and people who know. In any conflict, you need to understand what the other person is dealing with. If you're a leader, you need to know how that person consumes information and content from you. Because if you're delivering messages to them and it's going over their head, or it doesn't feel right, or they just don't get it, then what's the point? You need to help yourself to help them. It's a two-way street. Look up the Think, Know, Feel model to dig deeper on that.
- Be strategic about how you brand yourself. If you don't brand yourself, someone else will. If you're not doing it for the benefit of what you want your legacy to be, then someone else is going to scoop you up and start getting you to do things that are going to help with their legacy as opposed to yours.
- Don't network for the sake of networking. Find the right people and keep meeting them over and over. Because if you have a really strong base network, they're going to be referring you to people left, right and centre because they know you

inside-out. Don't spend your time doing ten networking events a month when you can do two or three that have a real and massive impact.

BIO

Megan is a Scottish lass who has made Western Australia home since 2012. She considers herself fortunate to have held several executive positions in the not-for-profit sector, including a CEO stint, predominantly in agriculture, international education, Indigenous and mining sectors. She is a proud gin snob, beach bum, book clubber but she is widely known as a personal brand strategist.

In 2019 she took the leap from a well-paying, stable career into entrepreneurship and started Relevant because she wanted to help more people build impactful legacies, they could be proud of. With a background in branding and psychology, Megan has the knowledge and skills to understand what you are trying to achieve and the means to help you do it. Her mission to ensure that you are reaching for goals that align with what you need and want. Not goals conjured up by cognitive biases. Megan helps remove friction that is preventing you from getting to the next level and offers space to safely talk about the ideas running around in your head to help you critically assess them

relevantbusiness.com.au
linkedin.com/in/meganmacneill

MIKEL SANZ PEÑA
CHOOSE YOUR OWN ADVENTURE

Nothing ever ends well for anyone in conflict when your goal is only to be right.

Sometimes the only place to do Zoom calls was in the bathroom – it had a lockable door, and the acoustics were great, it became a running joke and brought humour to our meetings.

TELL US ABOUT WHAT YOU DO AND WHAT YOU LOVE ABOUT WHAT YOU DO

I have been working in the energy and offshore industries all my professional life, starting as an engineer. It took five years to find a true call in the contracts and legal side; letters, words and relationships have always appealed and it turned out that was my professional forte. In one early and key interview, the decision-maker confided, 'We aren't after a brain on a stick, we've already seen you ticked all the boxes from university, what we need is someone who can work with others – not someone who will cause a strike in the control room.' Well, it can't have been that bad, as a career meandered towards heavy construction and maintenance contracts. Rather than engineering, per se, it was contracts and seeing how they are powerful forces, but also how much conflict can emerge from them. Working in this space I could see how quickly disputes snowballed at all levels, and I also learnt what can be done to stop a fire from catching and spreading. One realisation was that contracts can be a force for good and that they can be a tool for mediation, because when you've got something written down, perhaps more so under common law, or some set of rules, you can help parties meet a solution. When you help parties find a solution that they have come up with, it's a very gratifying situation.

TELL US A LITTLE ABOUT HOW COVID IMPACTED WHAT YOU DO AND HOW YOU ADAPTED

We've all experienced a similar transition, haven't we? From, 'I'll have so much more work-life balance,' to the lines of work and personal blurring. Sometimes, quite physically, with the boundaries of your literal home and your literal (home) office impinging on each other.

Perhaps it's less interesting to look at what we went through than where we ended. It can be healing to share the highs and lows of what we all seem to have gone through, while adapting to the new 'not normal'.

I can tell you that before COVID, I never thought I would have meetings on a bike or that a drink with my father-in-law at 6pm on a Friday could taste so good.

It's a little cliché but making those little gestures of, 'The weekend has started – where is the nearest drink?' could have a powerful effect. Contrast that with your former extending Friday evening which, on not-so-rare an occasion, became yet another conversation about work with colleagues at the pub.

That's not to say we don't miss the healthy bonding with people with which we spent so much working time with, however, skipping those opportunities did offer a bridge to a better weekday-weekend boundary. In my experience, the reverse had previously been true, where the workday-evening boundary seemed to be a constantly moving target.

Once the work-from-home/work-from-anywhere stigmas and privileges disappeared, with all of us in the same boat, we were soon able to realise what our everyday WFH colleagues and friends of old (freelancers, stay-at-home parents, to name a few) had told us before, 'It's great, I'm fortunate, and I do it because it works for me … but I wouldn't wish it on my worst enemy!' I'd say that's one of my biggest takeaway from adapting to life during and after COVID.

And so hopefully, we, at some point, stopped feeling the pressure of being on 'screen' and FaceTime and started to introduce healthy routines into our meetings. However, this also made it hard at times to engage with the other party.

From the beginning, COVID has impacted us in many different ways. It isn't all about remote work, but it has been more difficult to relate to others in the same way as pre-COVID. When you're not sharing all those physical moments, travelling and doing the work face to face, when you're not sharing a meal and going through those routines, you're not interacting in the same way. In the past we may have thought that stuff was sometimes overkill, but looking back, when you are away from your family and doing those 'routines' with your colleagues, you create goodwill. We've certainly had to adapt to the way we interact with others and as we start to come together physically again, we will have to adapt back, but this too will be different. We won't be able to 'switch off' the mute button. We can't wriggle out of the face-to-face interactions in the same way. We will have to relearn how to manage different personalities.

TELL US ABOUT DEALING WITH CONFUSION, CHANGE AND CONFLICT SINCE WE'VE BEEN IMPACTED BY COVID

I come from a part of the world, the Basque Country in northern Spain, with a bit of what some would call a collective intergenerational trauma, where sadly, when a conflict begins, participants often seek to be 'right' – all the time. When one party becomes entrenched in wanting to be right, you never know where that will end up. It often feels there is no end to that and that no resolution possible. When you've grown up with this approach as children and seen the high cost of conflict on adults, it can give you a different perspective, not only on societal but also professional conflict.

It's something I've seen impacting companies, especially

technical companies and engineers, because we scientists and engineers have been educated with an approach that there is 'one truth'. Engineers and scientists really want to be wrong (which is not dissimilar to wanting to be right – hold on with me here, it should make sense eventually) because what they've been taught is that this is how the scientific method works out solutions: weed out the wrongs until there is nothing else left. There is one best answer and you need to look for the truth. This approach can be very dangerous in a conflict situation, which may be the reason why it can be a challenge to be mediating in this context.

One of the hardest parts of dealing with any conflict used to be bringing people to the table. Once you got quarrelling sides to feel safe about their issue and to progressively open themselves to the other side, then half the job was done. There was often a 'two steps back for every three steps forward' approach, but you had a feel for when you were making progress. Importantly, it wasn't hard to spot car crashes and derailing conversations, so you were able to do something about them!

In these confusing and changing times, however, getting someone to listen wasn't nearly as much of a problem as, indeed, getting any clue about the level of engagement (or disengagement). We've had to develop new ways of assessing the dispute and participants and checking progress.

Monologues and crowded, faceless meetings started to become the norm. We were getting twenty-plus people in a meeting. It became easy to over-invite as we were trying to create opportunities for wider engagement, but this overcrowding made it difficult to know if anyone was listening. One of the first things we noticed is how the previous preconceptions of the approach to meetings changed, based on different personalities. All of a sudden, introverts became vocal, the more gregarious were quiet, and those of an agreeable nature stopped cooperating. I definitely feel that these factors have had an impact on the negotiations. Why? Perhaps that's for another forum, but what we needed and actioned was a trial-and-error adjustment of the setting: chronometers and a balanced set of interventions for a start. We had to adapt to emerging needs of participants.

TELL US ABOUT THE CRAICS, CROCODILE TEARS AND STANDOUT MOMENTS FROM THE LAST FEW YEARS

Locked in a hotel room with family for a long stretch of time, I was struggling to find anything resembling a work environment that was conducive to hard negotiations. While the topic at hand was hard and a lot of tough conversations had already been had, we kept making a point of switching cameras and keeping in close, cordial contact. At one point the counterpart became visibly overworked, obviously putting in more than their fair share of hours. Starting with an exhausted look and what I thought would not be a very unproductive session, I welcomed him to my new improvised office. The light was definitely not great, and it was not furnished with the plushest seat, but hey, it did have great acoustics; I was working from an (empty!) bathtub. The large ensuite bathroom was the only quiet place in the apartment, with a lockable door. It could have been because of good old schadenfreude (seeing another's discomfort), toilet humour or simply out of surprise, but my counterpart found this a lot funnier than it should have been. And it didn't just lighten the start and duration of many negotiations, it became a recurring joke that we later used to ease a distended environment, when having difficult exchanges with multiple sides at loggerheads.

There have been so many new things to learn in terms of how we manage negotiations and certainly crocodile tears have been used in different ways to try to influence outcomes. We had two parties at odds, and we were acting as an informal mediator. Even remotely, one party would not show their faces without a mask. They also ensured their key person was less visible and positioned them behind the camera when answering questions and giving tips to the interlocutor. The whole scene was meticulously arranged, and together with strategic switches turning the microphone on and off, it made it nearly impossible to manage the interactions. I use the term 'crocodile tears' in this mediation, because at some point in the conflict between these two parties, we ended up meeting their management and it became clear they were all very comfortable speaking English, which we had not thought was the case previously. What we were seeing were different negotiation tactics including 'culture' and 'language' to position and leverage.

One thing that stands out for me, working remotely, is the response elicited from people when we finally meet me in-person, after hours of online meetings. It never gets old, and in great part is to do with height perceptions. I'm 1.63m and often work with companies, clients and professionals in countries where people have an average height closer to 2m. The faces of shock upon the first 'second' impression always works to crack a joke. Well, at least remotely, no-one is getting a sore neck, that's for sure!

SHARE YOUR HACKS, INNOVATIONS OR LEARNINGS THAT HAVE EMERGED FROM THIS TIME

How do you get people into a meeting on time in a busy online world? I often start an online meeting four minutes after the hour and finish seven minutes before the hour; it may seem silly, but find it helpful. Yes, mass remote working has made logging in and out of meetings easier, but how many of us are present in mind from the start? By sending a couple of adjustments to an invite, it makes people re-read or, at least, consider their attendance. Then, by using whimsical durations (15:04-16:23, see you there!), it can lighten the mood, create intrigue and spur some 'connection' conversation. It also allows for difference – those who are running late suddenly are on time, and those who are organised get a moment to have their coffee! All of this gives parties breathing space and helps ease them into the difficult conversations.

Another innovation we have adopted, and works well for us, is to visually use diagrams to capture and clarify what is occurring within the negotiations. We don't see a lot of other practitioners doing this, but it allows us to capture the chatter. With lawyers and engineers, it has allowed me to 'cut through' the positional fighting and can help to kill off unproductive conversations. This is obviously easier in-person, but good technology and screen-sharing has enabled us to continue doing this in a useful way.

Using diagrams, it forces us to simplify complex information to create more clarity. We have had engineers telling us, 'Oh, my Word. All these years, the lawyers couldn't explain it to me, but it was so simple.' While some conversely lawyers have confided, 'Does anyone really understand that chart?' and, 'Frankly, I can't think of anything more explosive than two lawyers armed with a calculator.' What we are trying to find is the common ground. 'Let's see how much of this you can agree on.' If we can help parties agree on fundamentals of the situation, sometimes, it is an easier step to agreement.

LOOKING FORWARD, WHAT DO YOU THINK MIGHT BE SOME LASTING TRENDS OR INFLUENCES?

As we move forward, it's become all about remote working, hasn't it? We don't believe it was an intention, so how did we end up here? How are we dealing with this challenge of creating connections, trust and goodwill? We don't have an answer for that, but we do think those moments of humour, lightness and connecting simply as 'humans' are key.

A great lasting trend we forecast is finding a way to trust in each other without an established set of codes. To be specific: meetings, gatherings and chattery seemed to have morphed into calls (with or without video), email chats and lots of instant written communications in various formats.

We have a story that comes with a mix of humour and dread, as just one example of a new challenge leading to a possible trend.

There we were, all set up: attendees in place, apologies sufficiently in advance, not an ungodly hour and even a room with a view, sunny weather ordered and delivered, and fresh coffee steaming on the table. A few couldn't make it on what would have been an unavoidable weekday business trip pre-COVID.

The meeting was had, exchanges traded and minutes were taken. Not an eventful meeting, but as positive as one could wish, with all participants engaged in pleasantries and the odd joke. All in all, there was progress, and some results were patent. In customary fashion for such a relevant and prescriptive meeting, the host had taken shorthand notes of the meeting.

Fast-forward to the days after and the minutes were exchanged: the tension was not only *not* defused by a literal transcript of the participants' conversation, it suffered quite a setback as participants were concerned about the accuracy of the transcript! Admittedly, the parties had not explicitly request nor communicate the style of minutes that would be taken. What was *different* was that the surprising detail of the transcript chipped away at the confidence achieved in the meeting, which could have literally been a *recording!*

The takeaway in this is that the critical balancing act of maximising professionalism and ensuring mutual trust has changed. We ask ourselves, is it harder now, or were we overly ceremonious in the pre-turbulent times?

One way or another, COVID or not, technology is changing the way we do business. Whether we are keen to embrace it or reluctantly adopting it, adding to the two parties and the mediator in the 'room', there is now a fourth guest: ignore it at your peril, for the mere thought of what it could be used for may open cracks in the most solid of relationships.

The other very topical questions we see emerging into the future are the increase in focus and visibility of society values and expectations about environment, sustainability and our impact on the world within the large-scale renewable energies industry. There are a lot of pitfalls and complexities to this conversation, but the question is, 'How are the societal changes impacting the business of large-scale renewables, especially the large carbon-producing entities, and the very visible, massive infrastructure of the offshore wind industry?' In the past, negotiations were more one sided, 'We are doing this and it's about money,' which meant there was a tad less nuance to conflict. Now there are multiple layers to disputes. Companies may be losing money and negotiations might focus on 'how do we complete these projects on budget?' Often the disputes are between developers and people down the supply chain or between two developers sharing an investment. Sadly, conflict can morph into witch-hunting and competing interests from every side. Positions can polarise between profit and people, and the challenge of financial realities, which full circles to cause yet more conflict potential.

This takes us back to one hopeful core insight; 'When your goal is solely to be right, there is no productive outcome for anyone.' So, when we enter complex multicultural environments, different political systems and layers of values and principles, we have to remember that not everyone thinks the same and that's okay.

YOUR TIPS FOR DEALING WITH PEOPLE DYNAMICS DURING CONFUSION, CHANGE AND CONFLICT

- Forget your preconceptions on personality types. There have been multiple essays and opinions on this topic, but it cannot be understated – we have all changed! From the camera switch-offs to the pressures of returning to physical presence, to meeting outside work to keep relationships and overworking, COVID has thrown a spanner in the works of adapting to others and we must find ways to adjust the way we communicate.

    For instance, we had a client who was usually driven and very vocal during negotiations. It worked for them, but they really struggled to engage as we shifted to online. We had to work hard to get them to contribute, they just weren't engaging. We had to find ways to ensure they were contributing to decision-making.

    We have seen both the worst and best of people responding, adapting and adjusting in the ways we meaningfully communicate. Part of our job is working with personalities to try to understand them and to know all this training we've received is not useless. For me, COVID has certainly highlighted the depth of how much there is still to learn about how people interact in conflict.

- Prioritise forgiveness above 'being professional'. We have all been under immense pressure, but we tend to measure others based on our experiences. We don't always know the extent to which a confusing situation may have tipped others over the edge and everyone has their own challenges.

    We were working with a party and found that they were

increasingly dealing with internal fighting. Frustrations boiled over and mudslinging between people on the 'same side' made moving forward impossible. By stopping to understand what was happening behind the scenes, we discovered that one of their team was dealing with a severe occupational injury which was getting worse. They had little home support with children, and the pressure was extreme. We all were reminded that we were judging from our own prism, instead of bringing forgiveness.

It pays to be forgiving, to perhaps not enforce the rules of professionalism at every turn, to allow us to be more human. Although we must acknowledge that professional rules are integral to work and are there for a reason, we also need to recognise that, sometimes, we all need a break when times get tough.

- Ensure everyone has a say in the format of how we communicate. Previously accepted ways of work have not fully been replaced and so we can and may find that peers, colleagues and clients adapt at a different pace and with inventive or traditional approaches. We all need to accept that there is no one homogenous 'new normal'.

Back home where I come from, we talk about the *battle for the story*: a struggle in which broadly two sides try to persuade a multipolar society (made of more than two sides) about which account is more truthful and more just. But really 'nobody' wins in such a struggle. And the history's story becomes just that – a story. As peacemakers, we want to look at different perspectives of the story, or perhaps not make a story at all. We've learned that when parties focus only on the 'fairness' of their own story, then constructive outcomes are rare and a long way off. Our role as mediators is really to help people understand each other better, to see their conflicts as more than a battle and to make it possible for them to see a joint way forward.

BIO

Mikel is an offshore wind dispute professional who brings more than fifteen years of deep experience having become a FIDIC dispute resolution and avoidance specialist in supply, installation, EPC and operations/service contracts in the offshore environment. Whilst Mikel is an engineer at heart, he has spent much of his career managing contracts and disputes including ten years as contracts and commercial manager in the North Sea and Taiwan for key suppliers headquartered across the globe. He now specialised as an offshore wind contracts and dispute management professional and has been instrumental in facilitating several deals to an industry-leading level. He helps raise QHSE awareness and imagines that he brings a project no-nonsense edge and is often described by clients as a structured innovator.

In 2022 he helped establish Tornasol, a company that believes contracts are a force for good and that mediation is a tool to help bridge differences between organisations and parties within the offshore wind industry. With an understanding that disputes are best settled through cooperation, they provide assisted mediation, contract analysis and commercial account management services.

tornasol-cm.com
linkedin.com/in/s-mikel

MING JOHANSON
TIME TO THINK

As a leader you are not a punching bag for others' conflict, rather you are the support structure, the scaffolding that supports people through conflict, change and confusion, you show them how to best proceed. You provide a safe place. Mostly people in conflict are just struggling to move forward.

You are not meant to be the punching bag for other people's conflict – but you can create the safe place for them.

TELL US ABOUT WHAT YOU DO AND WHAT YOU LOVE ABOUT WHAT YOU DO

I'm a nerd, amongst other things, and I tend to push a lot of buttons on the internet. In 2019 I was an award winner at the Women in Tech awards, and I talk in the media about all sorts of things ranging from technology to social media, privacy and cybersecurity. I'm also a mentor for Startup Weekend, where I usually yell at people and talk them out of mortgaging their homes for their, as yet, unvalidated new business idea. I've been running my digital marketing agency called Marketing Jumpstart for twelve years now, and prior to that I was a business development manager in a national telecommunications company.

I'm also passionate about mental health and have been an ambassador for R U OK? Day, for the past five years. I speak regularly on the topics of mental health, suicide and suicide prevention, as I have my own lived experience in mental health, which I share through that journey.

I've got lots of experience in many different areas. I really love to solve complex problems, because by simplifying them you discover they are not so complex after all. What makes things difficult is people and ego. What I love about my business is that I have built a business that is psychologically safe for me, and then by proxy, have created a psychologically safe business for other people, who typically may not be in a normal business realm.

TELL US A LITTLE ABOUT HOW COVID IMPACTED WHAT YOU DO AND HOW YOU ADAPTED

My greatest challenge with COVID was probably not what people would think. I went down a very particular route, making decisions that went against all the advice everyone was giving me at the time. At the very beginning of the pandemic, the advice was to cut your team, slim down, downsize – you know, just streamline and automate. Instead, I went down the road of actually employing all my subcontractors. I gave them jobs, which in turn, gave them security, because in my mind, I could see that security would be imperative to my team's mental health.

I have a diagnosis of PTSD anxiety disorder, and when there is chaos, for me, that is my calm place. For most people, chaos causes stress, whereas I'm like, 'Okay, what can I control?' I become hyper-focused on the things in my environment that I can control. And looking forward to what is going to happen in the future. I could see quite a number of things that were going to happen that would require security for my team. I chose to go against an overwhelming amount of advice from my accountant, from my advisors, my coaches and pretty much every other business owner I was talking to at the time. They all called me crazy. They all said that I was making some serious, potentially mentally-unhinged decisions. But I did it anyway. And now, just over two years after the pandemic, I have a team of seven employees. We've grown both personally and professionally. We've been more financially secure in our business than any other time for the past twelve years. And our clients are more secure. The ethos of the thought process was very much around, 'If my team are secure, the business is secure and our clients will be secure.' And it's played out. It's been fun and it's paid off.

Though adapting during COVID there were still lots of difficulties that came up in that despite everybody thinking, *Working from home is great,* there are lots of team dynamics that come up, with people acclimatising and bringing their own bullshit from other jobs too. So there was a lot of navigating to do.

TELL US ABOUT DEALING WITH CONFUSION, CHANGE AND CONFLICT SINCE WE'VE BEEN IMPACTED BY COVID

I think many people have had a massive identity crisis during this time, accentuated by the pandemic. Let me explain …

When people talk about me, the word 'authentic' gets thrown around a lot. It's not like I'm intentionally running around going, 'I'm gonna be authentic.' But I am just being myself, and like all of us, I'm flawed – a flawed human being. I make terrible decisions. Sometimes, incredibly risky decisions. But I'm open and honest, and a lot of people struggled with that.

At the beginning of the pandemic, I saw many business leaders struggling to be honest with their team, 'We're fine, we're okay,' just didn't work anymore, and they were being pushed into a space of honesty and openness. Business leaders had to adapt to change.

Being the nerd that I am, there were a lot of businesses I'd been speaking to for close to ten years, about working on their digital presence. It was a constant conversation for me, but they didn't see it as a priority, 'We'll look at it next financial year,' or, 'It's in our five year plan,' were regular responses.

They were like, 'That's just a bit of noise over there. We'll deal with that later. Right now we've got to deal with front of house.' And then suddenly, they didn't have a front of house because they had to close the doors for the first time. We had a lot of clients come to us asking, 'What do we do now? How can we make our business work on the internet?' It was like, they couldn't step through the physicality of their business into how that would look online.

We had one particular client who we helped out and supported through the pandemic. They are a family of chocolatiers, in business for over eighty years, with three generations of chocolatiers. Prior to COVID, they had a website, which is nice, but they'd made the sum total of $30 from their website sales. They'd never really pushed anyone to it and it wasn't making any money. In the first year of the pandemic, we made them something like $16,000, which they had not anticipated. It was unanticipated income, which was huge for them. I just spoke to them recently and their current conversation is, 'We want to close the retail store altogether, and just go for online.' They now have so much overwhelming evidence that they can actually make money from the internet. It was wild for me, because it was like, 'I've been beating this drum for a while guys.'

What's really fascinating to me is that there are still so many businesses in an avoidance pattern around digital. They still feel it's like Pandora's box. But I think all of that uncertainty is imagined uncertainty. Because everything online is measurable; every button click, every email form. You can measure how long people are on your website and what they are engaging with. There's so much certainty in what can be measured and tested. One of the things we say in our business is that we don't 'crystal ball gaze'. It's maddening but there's still a lot of people in our industry who say, 'We can get you *xxx* thousands of people to your website.' But that doesn't really mean anything. What will they be doing when they get there? What are they clicking on? What are they being driven towards? From our point of view, there's a real conversation about the customer journey. What do you want your customer journey to be like?

I feel there is still avoidance from the small business operator, they don't want to acknowledge who they truly are. They want to pretend to be something they're not. There's a misalignment with their authentic brand versus their actual brand. They are then attracting the wrong clients and wondering why. You'll be surprised at how many people out there will be your client just for being yourself.

I'm the biggest example of that, right? I run around like a wild woman on the internet, looking for different ways of thinking. It seems wild to me that nobody else is doing it. There're probably companies out there that are, but it it genuinely feels like nobody else is doing that.

I think a lot of us have worked in those large organisations that beat out individuality. They tell you to leave your problems at the door. You just have to show up and do your job. The work is the work. People spend a lot more time masking and pretending to be something they're not and how they are feeling, and by the time they finish their workday, they're exhausted. They're mentally fatigued to the point that they don't enjoy their lives. Right now we're hearing terms like 'quiet quitting'.

For us, in our business, we're actively telling our team that we don't want them to be a workaholic. We don't want over-achievers. I appreciate where that comes from, but we figured out quite recently, in order to be the best employee fit for us, you have to be an over-achiever in your previous job, not in ours, because we will literally untrain you of that. We let our employees know they can push back and tell us that the deadlines need to change. We want open communication. This attitude allows everyone to step up to a higher level of communication, where everyone is open about their emotional state, about where they're at, about what's going on for them, what might be impacting their work and where they might need support. A lot of my team would advocate the fact that I regularly say, 'How can we support you?' as opposed to, 'Why didn't you do that?' Nothing good comes out of that kind of 'why' question. Nothing! Only if you want to immediately switch somebody into being the five-year-old who did something silly. Instead, flip that question into, 'How can the business support you and what resources do you need?'

There are a number 'why' questions that can actually cause conflict, especially in the post-COVID age where leaders are adapting to change. Those old expectations hold so much judgement:
- Why didn't you hit that deadline?
- Why aren't you working later/harder?
- Why didn't you deliver it to the exact version I had in my head but didn't communicate properly?

When we're faced with that style of leadership we end up putting ourselves and others under so much pressure, often asking of ourselves, 'Why aren't you perfect?'

In my opinion, it's outdated and conflict driven.

In our business, we've actually got rid of 'time' and the concept of a nine-to-five workday. That was partly beacuse everybody has different bio rhythms. I wake up at 4am, which not many people know, but I usually start my day at four because my body just decides to wake up then. Well, I could lie in bed for the next four hours, or I could just get up and be productive. For those first three hours of the day, it's pretty uninterrupted. I have a remote team that works across the country, so by 6am and 9am I'm working with the team. The attachment to a nine-to-five day just doesn't work when you're a remote company. But then, I don't know if it works at all anyway, because we have these stories that we attach to time. 'You're late,' well, are you? Why did you have to be there, or could you have sent an email?

I think one of the biggest changes through COVID has been that leaders have stepped up into being more open about their mental state. Because we all went through it. We've all gone through this pandemic. Certainly, in my own team, we shared the collective burden of what was going on for the team. Two of our team had long COVID and there were real challenges that came from that. At one point, our business had 75% of the team out of action, which is enormous for small business. For other leaders I was speaking to at the time, they were faced with the fact that they had an 'excuse' to be honest. 'We can be honest here, because we're all going through it. Everybody is experiencing this.' We were experiencing different versions of it but we could all just collectively take a breath. And that actually built trust with the teams. Because their teams were able to see their leaders as another flawed human being. And it made people feel safer in their workplaces, harnessing trust and a sense of connectedness.

That also leads to a sense of value alignment which has always been really important for our business. I've made decisions to get rid of clients on the basis of not aligning to our values. Anything that results in the sacrifice of my team's mental health has to go, that's my line in the sand. And that's actually been a difficult lesson for me because when you grow up in a violent environment, your line in the sand for yourself is not the same as for other people. You will draw that line a lot sooner for other people than you will for yourself. I've sometimes had to recalibrate for myself as well and go, 'Okay, this isn't acceptable. I wouldn't allow this behaviour for other people, so why would I allow it for myself?' A steep learning curve.

TELL US ABOUT THE CRAICS, CROCODILE TEARS AND STANDOUT MOMENTS FROM THE LAST FEW YEARS

I spoke earlier about things I was predicting in the future that were going to happen with the team, and one of the driving forces behind the decisions I made to employ them was purely around security. I saw that we were going to hit a rental crisis. At the time, we were at less than 1% rental vacancies available, and that would mean if any of my team were renting a home and asked to leave, they would struggle to find another place. Buying a home of their own needed to be an option, that's why I employed everyone so that they would have payslips and security and could prove they were financially secure. I didn't go down the road of casual, to then full-time, I went straight to permanent, again, against all advice. And so, in the second year of the pandemic, five of my six team at the time, had bought a house. That was amazing, and huge for me, especially considering I came from being homeless when I was seventeen. Being able to create jobs, security and an opportunity for people to buy their own home has been amazing. I still get choked up about it. It means so much to me that my team have that kind of security.

Someone recently joined us who has come from government work, and she said to me recently that the team maybe didn't really realise the full extent of the value of what they have in our business. I think they do, I just don't think they verbalise it. Having a conversation with another member of my team recently, he acknowledged that we've built something quite precious that needs to be protected. And the way that we protect it is to succeed. And if we succeed, our clients succeed, and everyone is succeeding … that's how we protect this. That's how we make it whole.

SHARE YOUR HACKS, INNOVATIONS OR LEARNINGS THAT HAVE EMERGED FROM THIS TIME

For me, it always comes back to mission, vision and values. There were a few points throughout the entire pandemic, where my team would roll their eyes into the back of their heads whenever I continued to bring up values. 'Alright, let's talk about our values. Let's recalibrate our values. Let's talk about our plan. Let's talk about our future.' We've just had another conversation about what the next twelve months will look like and reflected on what we've achieved in the last twelve months. And they're all like, 'Okay, well, we've cleared out clients that don't align, we've got all of our legals and terms of trade in order, and we're looking at different things that are protecting us as a business. But we're also doing really good work. And our clients have changed and evolved. And we're having fun.' So those mission, vision and values are real. There's a genuine truth you have to find in those things. Values, for me, have always been a driving decider as to whether or not I work for an organisation. So when I worked in telecommunications, in the job interview, I knew what the values were as I'd memorised them. And the moment I left was the moment they misaligned with their own values. One of their values at the time was, 'Our people and our customers are everything to us.' But then they turned their staff into numbers. And I saw their values were just words they had stuck on a wall.

Delegation is really important. It can also be a hard lesson, especially if you've been building a business on your own, because you're so used to just 'doing it'. And then when you hand it over, there's like a piece of your ego that you have to hand over at the same time. 'I don't know if you could do this as well I can.' But it's really about valuing your time differently. 'If you're time was worth $280 an hour, what would you stop doing?' Well, anything you're paying somebody less to do.

I've outsourced our own branding, because I know I would probably spend one hundred hours staring at it being obsessive and not getting anywhere. Whereas if I just hand over the trust to somebody else who is skilled at it, they'll do it in ten hours and ultimately cost me a lot less.

When it comes to conflict innovation, I think the biggest part is meeting people where they're at. And they're not always going to be involved in that conversation or necessarily emotionally present but it's important to treat individuals as individuals. Everybody is different. Everybody has a different story that they bring to a situation, and it's important to seek to understand where they're coming from.

The irony is, I realise I've been doing this for some time but was probably not consciously aware how I was dealing with it. In my mind, it really falls under leadership. For me, there's a necessity that you're going to deal with conflict at every stage of business. During any growth, we're dealing with conflict; some sort of chaos happens. It's either internal conversations or somebody's frustrated because they're not being understood. And the other person gets overwhelmed, because they're trying to understand, but communication falls apart. You just want everybody to get along and everybody should take the time to breathe and understand each other, right? Somebody I know recently referred to being the mediator in your own business, as being the punching bag, but you're not a punching bag. You know, what you are? You are the support structure; the core support that people feel safe enough to come to you and have a conversation. Because what they're really seeking is to figure out how to best proceed. They want to move forward. The conflict is really about the struggle to move forward.

I've given a few talks recently about unconscious bias, and I usually refer to money as an analogy, because money is not gendered and everybody has a different story about money. It's a good way to get people to push through that conversation and understand unconscious bias in all areas, and how it affects your decision-making and engagement with other people.

Another hack is the importance of self-care – I do my own internal work. I have psychologists, I have therapists, I have to show up for those conversations. And I have to make sure I'm not bringing all of my bullshit to that conversation as well. When I'm already dealing with two conflicting parties, I need to be the sensible one, and looking after my self is imperative, especially right now that we've gone through this pandemic. We are all fatigued. We are all burnt-out. We are all overwhelmed. We're all feeling it. Nobody has come out of this unscathed – nobody. I have yet to meet that person. Self-care is also about allowing yourself to take time to think. There seems to be a lot of processes in business that often ask their teams for immediate answers and I don't think people have the mental capacity to do that anymore. Certainly not right now, with all of the stress. They need time to think and they need time to breathe.

LOOKING FORWARD, WHAT DO YOU THINK MIGHT BE SOME LASTING TRENDS OR INFLUENCES?

Certainly, in our business, I think the lasting impact is the necessity for honesty and openness about where we're at, in our mental health and our wellbeing in our sensibilities and identity. I think that is imperative. And that's something that we do as a business very well. Just naturally, it's sort of been built into the DNA of the business, because it's in my DNA. I know that there are some people who have come into our business, and it doesn't work for them. They are they are looking to pretend to be something they're not. It gets revealed very quickly and doesn't fit.

Another lasting trend is moving towards things like working from home and a four-day work week. I think it's a necessity. When I look at it practically and how we run our business, I wonder how it would look if we were in an office. In an office, I think we'd have a lot more meetings that would probably be unnecessary. We'd be spending a lot more time around the watercooler and more time having lunches. We don't do any of that. And so, we're quite an efficient team for five days a week. Technically, I'm actually getting far more work out of my team than I would expect from four days. I'm not asking them to do five days' worth of work in four days, I'm asking them to do four days' worth of work, because that's how much work I think we actually do. Somebody asked me what our capacity for growth is, and I responded that we're at 50% capacity. We actually have a lot of space for growth, we can take on a lot more work.

Moving forward in the digital marketing world, I think, is to be willing and able to embrace whimsy. Like being whimsical and having fun and being able to be genuine and open. In our team, we all have a similar dark sense of humour. Just recently someone asked, 'What's the ultimate career path?' and somebody sparked up with, 'Well, the ultimate career path for *everyone* is death.' We laughed!

The digital world gets overcomplicated very quickly. You don't have to be everywhere. Just pick one platform and get good at it. That's the advice I've given for over twelve years now. It's still the same. Just pick one and get good at it. If you're trying to split yourself between seventy different platforms, you're just going to burnout. Video content is always top of mind because we're connecting through it more, and TikTok is killing it, doing extremely well at the moment. But importantly, again, where is your audience? And is that where you should be? LinkedIn is great for professional connection. Figure out where your audience is, and where they're making decisions, and spend your time there. That's the crux of it.

YOUR TIPS FOR DEALING WITH PEOPLE DYNAMICS DURING CONFUSION, CHANGE AND CONFLICT

- Self-care. You really have to check your own mental health before you get engaged in anybody else's stuff. Otherwise, you will only perpetuate drama. Make sure you engage in whatever self-care looks like for you. It could be meditation, it could be therapy (I'm a big advocate for therapy). It could be

you having a routine of self-care but find what works for you.
- Processes – that's a big one for us. When are processes are flowing, our values are in flow. If something is not working, how can we adjust or tweak the processes to support either the people doing it or the role within the business? Figure out the processes that support people. If you have a little instruction manual that says, *Hey, this is how we do it as a business*, then there's no argument as to whether or not it was done right or wrong.
- Check your language. What I mean by that is there's lots of words we use in our everyday language that are geared around pressure. They're phrases like, *have to, got to, need to, should, must* – coulda, shoulda, woulda! All of those things are designed to put us under pressure. And checking your language is not just about deleting those words, it's replacing them. Remember, there's nothing you *need to do*, there's nothing you *have to do*; they're nice ideas, but you don't have to do *anything*. You don't even have to get out of bed. It's just a good idea. You don't have to shower, but it'd be nice if you did. It's a choice, and remembering that it's a choice, you can choose to, want to and desire to do something. Using words like these changes the energy and the nature of what those conversations look like.

For me, one of the biggest outcomes of COVID for all of us is we have all gone through it. Our collective consciousness is connected in a way like never before. We've all been connected through this massive global event. I like to think that we're being prepared for space travel, but you know, these things allow us to be human. It's about remembering our humanity. People are going through a tough time, so just checking in on them and being genuine about that is about compassion and humanity – and we could all do with more of that!

BIO

Ming brings a wealth of experience having worked with businesses across the globe from training social media to managing (with her team) complex digital strategies that deliver tangible and desirable financial returns. She is dedicated to shaping the landscape for leaders to adapt management, sales, and marketing culture to fit into the modern-day world of hyper-connectivity. Ming is CEO at Marketing Jumpstart, director of media at DDD Perth, a co-facilitator in Startup Weekend Perth and a regular Australian media commentator as a tech evangelist on a range of topics in mental health, social media and technology. She was recently recognised and awarded for her ongoing contribution to the technology industries in the 2019 Women In Technology Tech [+] 20 Awards. Ming is also a passionate mental health Ambassador for R U OK? Day.

marketingjumpstart.com.au

PAUL SILLS
THE GLOBAL TOUCH

Increasingly I have seen pain expressed as polarisation and difference spark conflict rather than curiosity. Unless we as mediators help come together in dialogue, we are not going to be able to get the changes we need into the future.

Working in conflict resolution is like an endless academic and practical study of the human dynamic and all the elements that bring us together or pull us apart. In our work, we constantly come up against psychological issues, and I rush to tell people we're not therapists, but I have to use my knowledge of fields like neuroscience and psychology alongside my heavy legal background.

TELL US ABOUT WHAT YOU DO AND WHAT YOU LOVE ABOUT WHAT YOU DO?

As a barrister in New Zealand, I spent many years working on mostly commercial disputes. About 14 years ago, I became interested in mediation and started my own practice, which has grown over the years. I had expanded a little into Australia and internationally, and now my family and I have relocated to London, so I'm based in the UK, with my primary focus on mediation and facilitated negotiation. I have a commercial dispute resolution focus, but I also work on the relationship side of negotiation and mediation. I tend to be involved earlier in the lifecycle of a dispute than most commercial mediators would.

I love learning and teaching, I think that's part of my personality type, and for me, my everyday work is about combining the two. Working in conflict resolution is like an endless academic and practical study of the human dynamic and all the elements that bring us together or pull us apart. In our work, we constantly come up against psychological issues, and I rush to tell people we're not therapists, but I have to use my knowledge of fields like neuroscience and psychology alongside my heavy legal background. It sounds a little cliché, but I just love the fact that every day in a mediation is a new opportunity to learn about people, and invariably learn about yourself, as you are reflecting on your learnings. I love sitting in that conflict space and being able to help people. It's a rare day in mediation where I don't get to reflect on something about myself.

Conflict is a huge part of all our lives and is always an opportunity to learn and to change direction, creating a fresh approach to how we look at things. It doesn't matter whether it's a husband and wife dissolving a marriage, or two CEOs of multinational billion dollar companies, conflict is conflict, and the drivers, the challenges to our identity, and ego getting in the road - all of these things are apparent, to various degrees in all of those conflicts. A family dispute, a shareholder dispute or a corporate dispute don't look that different when you break them down. Humans in conflict, are humans in conflict.

TELL US A LITTLE ABOUT HOW COVID IMPACTED WHAT YOU DO AND HOW YOU ADAPTED?

We've all had to go through a number of different phases, adapting to COVID. I guess, the initial phase was one of absolute disbelief. We were adjusting to a world that 'locked down'. I had just been in the UK visiting my family, dropping our daughter back to school after we'd had to go all the way back to New Zealand to get her visa sorted out. Flying back to New Zealand alone once they were settled, I was going through a lot of uncertainty, knowing that the UK was about to lock down and not really knowing what was happening in New Zealand. I had been focused on my family as opposed to what challenges might face my practice, and returning mid-March 2020, within a week of getting back, we had locked down.

Personally, it was an enormous challenge, because all of a sudden, my wife and two children were on the other side of the planet and there was a great deal of uncertainty as to when I might see them next. My personal experience was very much paralleling what we were looking at professionally. In dispute resolution, there was a significant level of uncertainty, along with fear and anxiety about what we were now grappling with, and how we were going to deal with it. I questioned whether we were to just sit at home, do no dispute resolution, and just hunker down or were we to make significant changes and take everything online? I had fortunately been working with Zoom and Immediation, mediating online anyway, doing some international stuff. For me the transition to mediating online and having breakout rooms, and all those practical things, I had been doing anyway. I was probably a lot more comfortable about the professional side of things. The big adjustment, was having to deal with reality and being up to the task of helping people professionally, while my personal life was experiencing so much uncertainty. But, across the board, globally, we were all dealing with the same anxieties, which I think was a great leveler.

From what I saw initially, I was hopeful that the adaptation we were going to see with COVID was going to be a lot more compelling, in terms of our degree of collaboration around dispute. And I think we saw it briefly, but one of my lasting memories of COVID and working through it, is feeling somewhat disappointed that we were, obviously, not going to take this opportunity to change the way we approach things, long term. (Talking as the 'collective' we – as in the human species). I think we did short term. Early on, we did reasonably well and there was a degree of collaboration forced upon us because of COVID and all the uncertainty, where we just had to 'get things done'. Moving forward, my lingering disappointment and concern is that I haven't seen that level of collaboration last.

TELL ABOUT DEALING WITH CONFUSION, CHANGE AND CONFLICT SINCE WE'VE BEEN IMPACTED BY COVID?

(Have we gone backwards in some ways?)

I think we've struggled to find our feet post-COVID, and there's a variety of reasons for that.

One is the practical side of it, where there were different jurisdictions and countries, with various restrictions coming off at different periods. In New Zealand where I was based, they've only really freed up travel and general vaccination restrictions over the last two or three months. And in Hong Kong and now China of course, they're experiencing a new set of problems, dealing with the zero COVID policy. So on the practical side of it, with restrictions coming off, I feel moving out of COVID is a little bit staggered and stuttering.

From my perception, there's been a push back to face-to-face, 'in person' life; far more than the advocates of doing everything online thought during the COVID period. I talk to a lot to people here in London about their own work experiences, and everybody, even outside of the conflict realm, seems to have a real sense of wanting to get back in contact with people. We could talk for hours about the pluses and minuses of interacting online both personally and professionally, but certainly as a mediator, what I've seen is a really interesting look at human nature and the desire to be back in contact with people. I certainly felt that when I was mediating during COVID, online, it was with one hand tied behind my back. I've got a couple of projects at the moment where I'm still using online platforms and I still feel the same, because I miss the nuances and the richness of being in a room with people.

I think it's really important for conflict scenarios, that we get to be as real, as authentic and as transparent as possible, and that only happens when we're in a room with people and we get all the richness of body language and comments and signs of agitation; everything that goes into an understanding of the space that a person is in. Even with three dimensional cameras, new technology and all the stuff that's coming into practice now as a result of the pandemic, the online space doesn't replace the intuitive side of what we do as practitioners. After a period of confusion, there's almost like two definitive groups; the online camp and not-online camp. I think we've all settled down a bit now, after the panic of the pandemic, and that's led to more in-person situations. For me, that has huge benefits as a mediator and that's the environment I want to work in; I want to sit around the table with people.

There's probably not been a shift in the 'type' of conflict work we've been doing but I think COVID has introduced the world to a new type of conflict and a new type of dispute; disputes that affect the human race as a whole. That was the fundamental change. It took us all time to adjust to the fear, the anxiety, the uncertainty and protection of family, through to, 'Okay, what does this mean long term for practice? What does this mean long term for commerce, business and international trade?' I feel at the moment we're seeing quite a traditional set of disputes. I think what the world will be going through over the next decade or so, is an intense focus on climate, on water issues, supply chain, and these sorts of things. These are the disputes that affect us across the globe. And so, if there are lessons to be learned from COVID, it's in how we approach conflicts that have such a long tail, that have an almost unimaginable list of stakeholders engaged in them. So that's where I see parallels moving forward. So for me, the pandemic was very much the start of a new regime of disputes that we will be dealing with, for a very long time to come.

It is very much a new chapter, and they won't all be about a pandemic, or medical in nature, but the global touch of these issues is the similarity.

TELL US ABOUT THE CRAICS, CROCODILE TEARS AND STANDOUT MOMENTS FROM THE LAST FEW YEARS?

A lot of my stuff over the last couple of years has been very personal. As I mentioned, my wife and children were living in the UK, and they had a really, really tough time. I was in New Zealand having a much easier time of it, and many of us didn't understand the pressures the rest of the world were under. Vanessa, and the children, went five weeks and never left the apartment. The kids never stepped over the threshold, because no one knew what was going on. In New Zealand I was dealing with my dad who had Alzheimer's, but he was still on the farm, and we decided that was the safest place for him. I spent every weekend with him. I'd finish work on Friday and drive to his place. At the time, we weren't allowed to drive around the country, but I had a dispensation so I could care for him, keep him safe, run the farm, then go back to work. The standout story for me through COVID, was just the enduring nature of getting on and dealing with what I needed to deal with, and I saw that in others too. I guess my biggest concern, post-COVID, for all of us, is how much mental health and well-being has come to the fore during COVID. And how much mental health played a role in any dispute I was assisting on, in areas where you would never have thought those issues would be popping up. We talk a lot about long-COVID in terms of the medical issues, and I understand that, but for me, long COVID is mental health. We are a connected species, and neuroscience has proven we thrive on connection, and to suddenly find ourselves in a disconnected world, has turned a lot of situations into conflict situations. I don't think we've seen anywhere near the end of that, and I don't think we've seen anywhere near the true effect of that.

The last few years has brought into view many things that we don't do well in society, like, dealing with vulnerability, conflict and the stress of leadership. It's just accelerated them all, to the forefront of everybody's experience. As dispute practitioners, we now see people no longer able to hold back their emotions, or hold it within themselves, despite their best endeavors, and to their great embarrassment. While that's how we've been brought up in the Western world, the cracks in our armour are now showing, and of course, as dispute practitioners, we reach out to that vulnerability, because we want to encourage and help people in that space.

It seems like the 'powers that be' don't want to acknowledge the depth of the issue of Mental Health in society. Everyone is in a state of confusion about how they feel mentally, you know, burnt out and exhausted, but too many people haven't got help with that or even feel comfortable enough about seeking help. To me, it's a massive issue simmering under the surface. I don't think, globally we are going to see much of a reprieve from the pressure of change. There are too many issues stacking up; the cost of living crisis, inflationary pressures, climate, what's happening in Ukraine, as well as the mounting pressure between China and the Western world.

I feel that being unable to talk about mental health can lead to people's pain being expressed in more aggressive ways. Because we have such a tradition in our culture of blaming and finger pointing, directing attention away from ourselves, we can end up creating a louder, more polarised challenge to the things in life that we don't agree with, or don't understand. As in, if I'm backed into the corner, I'm going to come out swinging. If mentally I'm exhausted, I'm fatigued and I'm scared, but I can't express that even to myself, so it has to manifest somewhere, and that's usually in a person's behavior towards others. Because if you leave it inside, it's going to blow you apart. So, we find the group that is diametrically opposed to our interests and pick on them. I think that's part of what of what we are seeing. We're finding a tribe of like-minded people and our thoughts are 'validated' by them. And we've been provided the tools to do it through social media and politics. Everywhere you look now, there's a polarisation effect going on. And it becomes a self-fulfilling prophecy, because people are encouraging each other. The political polarisation is encouraging social polarization - that's been happening for about twenty years now, but it's been accelerated by COVID.

This puts us at risk of making unhealthy connections, some that can fuel the worst sides of us. I read some terrible stuff recently on the rise of illicit sex crimes in the Philippines as a means for parents to get out of poverty. They become part of a 'tribe' where it seems 'Ok' if everyone else is doing the same.

It's important for the world to be having deep conversations about really horrible things, or really scary things, but we're avoiding all of them, and mediators have a role to play in bringing a critical skillset to the world. They're horrible, and distressing conversations for us, too, but I think as mediators, we step into that space, with the experience of having the courage to address those conversations. And often the mantra in my own head about being a mediator is, 'I want to have the most challenging conversation on the planet, with the people involved, in as calm and as empathetic a way as possible.' That's really the framework of what I want to achieve as a mediator because we aren't going to get change globally, on the tough social issues or the tough humanitarian issues or the tough climate issues, without that dialogue. Some of these conversations frighten the heck out of me too, but I am getting better and better at stepping into that space and saying, 'okay, but let's talk about that.'

After a day of tough conversations, I go home feeling like I've been run over by several freight trains! And I chuckle when my barrister friends think, a mediator's life must be 'pretty easy'. I'm not even going to bother having that discussion. I just say, 'Yeah, I'm basically in retirement.'

SHARE YOUR HACKS, INNOVATIONS OR LEARNINGS THAT HAVE EMERGED FROM THIS TIME?

Because of the personal experiences I've been through and what I see coming out of people in conflict during this period, it has made me a lot 'softer' on myself and on the people I work with. In commercial mediation especially, at times you have some pretty robust and direct conversations, but I think I do so now with a far greater understanding of the frailty and tragedy with which we all live. And how close to the surface that is for most of us and how quickly it can change. 'Softer' is not really a legally defined term, but I have developed a kinder, more gentle approach to my practice and very much to myself, which is its own achievement.

I'm a huge advocate now for awareness and mindfulness, both as a crucial part of what we do in our role as a mediator, and a crucial part of what we do as people. I think it is incredibly important for mediators to look after themselves and their mental health, particularly those who operate in highly emotionally charged areas, like family mediation and working with children. Those mediations can damage you if you're not careful.

For me, one of the great things I took out of COVID, was being part of an online group of mediators who would meet regularly. We formed great relationships within the group, and we could talk about some of the ugly stuff we had to deal with and some of the mistakes we'd made, all in a safe confidential learning environment. Going back to the point of connection, what we all need, as humans and most of us don't have, is a space and structure around us, with people that we trust and have absolute confidence in. A space where we feel comfortable enough and vulnerable enough to have the sort of conversations we need to get 'off our chest' and out of our system. Mental health issues aren't just a concern for the participants in conflict, they are there for the mediator as well. I believe a lot of people come into mediation, as if they are going into psychotherapy or psychology, looking for answers about their life. And if you take that into your work as a mediator, it's going to expand, it's going to be built upon by the challenges you see coming from other people, and that's going to have a really bad effect on you if you don't get on top of it.

Sadly though, post-COVID, the group no longer meets, and it's interesting, isn't it, how quickly, even a group of like-minded mediators, can fall away from these things when we don't perceive the need anymore. But in fact, the need to keep our own inner self healthy, is continuous. Taking care of ourselves is a daily exercise, things like meditation or journaling, sitting in nature, or walking in nature, exercise. All of them have validity. I guess that's an interesting parallel into what I've also seen with the COVID process.

In the first month of lockdown when I got back to New Zealand, I was talking with a friend of mine, who's a leadership coach, and we talked a lot about the fact that this (COVID) might be a *turning point for humanity*, in terms of collaboration and stepping away from self-interest and that sort of thing. It was within about 10 days when I messaged him and I said, 'No, it's not.' In that short time, I was already seeing signs on social media of people going back to self-interest and self-promotion. At the outset, everybody was in the same boat of fear, uncertainty and concern, but then not long after, 'Hello' we fell straight back into our old ways. And post-pandemic, as much as we've fallen back into some healthy ways, like in-person contact in dispute resolution, we've also fallen back into some very unhealthy ways. Our lifestyle, self-interest and polarisation, have all come rushing back.

So we've just fallen back into our own traps really quickly, and quite disappointingly, making our step up into the next set of global issues of climate and water perilous. It makes me feel like we haven't learned anything. From my point of view, after a pandemic and a shared global experience, I would have hoped there was a collective, 'Hey, while we're on a roll, let's get serious about climate change and let's actually put some meat in the sandwich, as opposed to a whole bunch of rhetoric.' As yet, we see none of that playing out around the world, none of it whatsoever, and I feel we've become more nationalistic and less globally focused than we've ever been since World War Two.

LOOKING FORWARD, WHAT DO YOU THINK MIGHT BE SOME LASTING TRENDS OR INFLUENCES?

I see a lot of work to be done, on many levels. There's a massive challenge coming because of this polarisation and intense individualisation. Even though we have seen some good intentions, trying to give people a voice, it feels as if it's also been a part of the polarisation effect. I see a massive clash between that and the reality, or the necessity, of collective action and how that plays out. As undramatically as it's possible to say this, I believe it will determine how, and if, we continue as a species. I think it really is that simple. We can carry on down the path as we are, but that's going to end up with a pretty catastrophic ending, and not too many generations into the future. Or we try to collectively salvage what we've got and make it right, again, as much as possible, which gives us a different future. But it is such a dramatically different future. And I don't know what side of it is going to win.

I read years ago, that the Hopi Indians in America had a sacred stone. Like a lot of indigenous people, they had some very amazing views into the future and the stone depicted a pathway, and at a certain point in time, the pathway separates. One pathway leads to a picture of happy old people collectively standing together, and the other pathway leads to a group of people whose heads are disconnected from their bodies. The symbology of us being at a crossroad and not knowing where we end up, seems to fit, and you can't overdramatise that. That is the reality of what I am seeing and feeling with the current way we sit on the planet. So, what is the natural conclusion of this increasingly partisan polarised way that we are living? What is the natural conclusion of the pathway that we seem to be on? It's not a conclusion I want to contemplate.

But I do remain an optimist in the face of all of that because life is still amazing. And it's beautiful, and people are incredible and capable of the most heart-wrenching kindness and beauty. However, I would have hoped, post-COVID, that we would be seeing more of that in our daily lives, and we're not. It's not really manifesting at the scale it needs to in economics, politics and society, in order to make a lasting change. Random acts of kindness will be lost in the noise unless people use them to grow and amplify them to pass them on. If we do that, incredible things can happen.

Looking forward, I believe conflict must become a healthy way of bringing about debate and change. But we're not approaching conflict, post-pandemic, in a healthy way at all and that's a big problem for us all. William Ury said, a long time ago, that *we need more, not less conflict*. But it's in our approach to dealing with conflict where the magic happens. When you mix conflict and diversity together, and I see it every day in London, which is why I love this city, it can be incredibly creative, incredibly dynamic. So it's not the conflict itself, it's not that we have a climate crisis, in many respects, *it's how we deal with it*. It's not that we have a mental health crisis, it's how we deal with it. That's where the learnings and the change come from. If we just repress, squash, cover up and wallpaper over the cracks of our mental health, like we have for generations, it's actually the definition of insanity. And the same with climate. So if we take exactly the same conflicts, and say, 'right, let's roll up our sleeves and talk about this, find a resolution and make a change, and all start walking to work, and appreciate that you'll get there a bit later, and all the things that are necessary to be a part of it,' incredible things happen. We can turn our cities into green havens, and capture our rainwater, and capture our grey water, and fix our infrastructure, so that our drinking water doesn't get lost, down broken pipes. We can start changing everything. But if you don't have the conversation, or you do have the conversation but it's not followed by action, then conflict will remain toxic.

YOUR TIPS FOR DEALING WITH PEOPLE DYNAMICS DURING CONFUSION, CHANGE AND CONFLICT

- Be true to yourself - don't try to do anything that you are instinctively uncomfortable with. That instinct in that instance,

will be telling you something for a reason. Don't try to be or do something that you aren't when you are in conflict, as it not a place to be anything but authentic.
- Try to be vulnerable when you are in conflict because you will often find that people will respond well to vulnerability. As an example, imagine you're sitting at a dinner table and you know half the people well, while the other half are complete strangers. If someone around the table during the night was to say something incredibly vulnerable, even if a total stranger, the response is unlikely to be negative. You will often find someone else will step in with their own vulnerability and share their example of it, because when we reach into that space, people are less afraid of wearing their heart on their sleeve. And in times of conflict, we need more of it.
- Try to be kinder and more understanding of other people's situations. There, but for the grace of *whatever you believe in*, we all go. The difference between a person with serious mental health or depression issues, and others, on a really bad day is a very fine matter of degree. And personally, COVID really brought that home to me. It was probably a lesson I needed to learn as a practitioner coming from 27 years at the bar, where you get a bit full of your own ego as a barrister. And I've certainly had most of that beaten out of me by life. But COVID was, again, a really tough reminder. It makes you realise that none of us sit on top of a pedestal or has all the answers. We are all under so much pressure.

What we truly need, is a big dose of human kindness.

BIO

A domestic and international arbitrator, mediator and barrister who draws on over 26 years of commercial and legal experience, Paul specialises in the early resolution of disputes both nationally and internationally for the benefit of all parties involved. With a diverse career that began in the RNZAF, Paul went on to become a Barrister and even took a break from law as CEO of a super-yacht construction company. Upon his return to law, he established his own mediation practice to compliment his commercial and civil court work.

Now based permanently in London, Paul brings a practical focus to his dispute resolution work and has combined his extensive legal experience and considerable business experience to offer negotiation, facilitation, and mediation services across the whole continuum of dispute resolution from helping people have better conversations through to appellate court work. Alongside this work he continues roles as director for several businesses.

He became a Fellow of the Arbitrators' and Mediators' Institute of New Zealand in 2019 (FAMINZ/ Med) and was recognised as one of the top 10 Mediators in New Zealand by Law Fuel.

paulsills.co.nz

ROAR THUN WAEGGER
NEGOTIATING WITH THE BRAIN IN MIND

I believe a lasting trend and a key success factor in tomorrow's workforce is human skills.

Like many people, I found myself with a decision to make during the early days of COVID. Do I wait and do nothing, see how things pan out, or do I take the jump, trust that moving forward will be ok. My choice was to jump forward, to take things online, to adjust, change and ultimately grow forwards better.

TELL US ABOUT WHAT YOU DO AND WHAT YOU LOVE ABOUT WHAT YOU DO

I started my business, WNI – Wægger Negotiation Institute, with negotiation training, advising and mediation in September 2017. I was doing a lot of training in Norway and other foreign countries. I did a job in Rome in February 2020, and we joked a bit about how this virus might spread from northern Italy to Rome. I flew home and did some onsite training, and again, we joked about it, but thought it was all going to be good.

Norway closed on 12 March and I had a rush of negotiation training cancellations. At that stage all our training was only onsite and my clients needed to protect themselves.

Together with a colleague, I was supposed to run a two-day training for a company, and we had it all prepared. We discussed, *What shall we do? Park and wait or jump straight into online training?*

We decided on the latter, and when I look back, that was a wise and strategic step.

I ran the first day of training with my only tool – my computer, including a camera and a microphone, of course. It was good that we were all freshmen in the online training world because I immediately felt the strong need for an upgrade, external widescreen, a good mic and an extra camera, among other tools. I felt I needed to present a professional look in addition to the content that we knew was good.

For me, the COVID adjustments I needed to make were a big awakening of how efficient negotiation training can be. When you look at the learning process and learning outcomes, the online training is as good as being on-site.

I asked my customers how they wanted to continue after

COVID restrictions were lifted, and several have continued with a mix. One customer ran two onsite trainings, and several participants chose to take the class online because they didn't need to travel and didn't need a babysitter. The way we have created an asynchronous training process ensures we avoid Zoom fatigue. Our participants can be present and focus on the training AND be available to do their business in the morning, during a long lunchbreak and immediately after. This works well for all parties, so it's a win-win solution.

TELL US A LITTLE ABOUT HOW COVID IMPACTED WHAT YOU DO AND HOW YOU ADAPTED

My immediate experience of dealing with change was to adapt to this new, *distanced* way of working during COVID. Since my customers, myself, and in fact, everyone else, was in the same situation, I didn't experience any conflict related to it. Of course, it hit hard on my wallet when almost everyone cancelled training agreements, but that didn't lead to conflict because we were all in the same difficult situation. People understood each other and went the extra mile to adjust and plan for continuation.

When I reflect, I do feel a level of conflict could have easily arisen from these cancellations for all parties, including myself, my customers, the venue owners and other service suppliers. From our work in the field of conflict resolution, we all know how difficult it is to de-escalate a conflict, so what happened?

I feel more of us understood each other and were able to take each other's perspectives, and I feel more were able to show and use empathy; a skill we try to teach in negotiation and mediation training and a tool we have available during mediation sessions.

Along with my colleague, Jason Liem, a psychologist from

Canada living in Oslo, one of the negotiation training concepts I run is, 'Negotiations with the Brain in MIND'. We have a session where we give the participants the ability to learn specific communication skills that target the neural circuits to shift mindsets from the reactive to the reflective. These skills can be used to help individuals manage themselves, situations and relationships. Two of those skills are cognitive lift and reframing, and once learned, they are in the participants' toolbox for shifting perspectives.

We know that shifting perspectives is difficult, especially when we are upset, as we normally are when in conflict.

I experienced that this 'normal' did not exist in its usual way when COVID hit us, but rather that many of us were able to understand each other and appreciate each other's situation.

My experience was that most people I did business with were able to use two core skills of a trained mediator's mindset – the ability to assess the opposite scenario and the ability to take another's perspective.

Mediators are trained to take a neutral, objective perspective on conflicts to help the parties overcome obstacles to resolution, including common judgement biases. During private meetings, mediators often encourage parties to look beyond their limited perspective and become open to collaborative solutions. The COVID situation showed me that many people have these skills and were able to use them.

I have written an article: 'Kareem Abdul-Jabbar «is hot for yoga» – lawyers should be hot for mediation training'. Here I wrote about lawyers who develop mediation skills and strengthen their traditional legal skills. I used an analogy with the basketball star, Kareem Abdul-Jabbar, because he was known for his special way of driving toward the basket, and he perfected his famous 'sky hook' skill. In addition, he regularly practiced yoga to develop his flexibility to perfect his 'sky hook'. This analogy can be applied to lawyers who have mediation training. Lawyers who develop mediation skills strengthen their traditional legal skills.

By training lawyers in a mediator role, a role in which the mediator impartially tries to help parties resolve a conflict, lawyers can develop habits of increased objectivity, compared to what they are asked to do. More lawyers just need to be pushed by their clients, then more lawyers will use those core skills of a trained mediator's mindset.

Dealing with change and conflict when we were first impacted by COVID gave me hope for humanity; we can change and collaborate much better than we normally do WHEN WE HAVE TO.

TELL US ABOUT DEALING WITH CONFUSION, CHANGE AND CONFLICT SINCE WE'VE BEEN IMPACTED BY COVID

Running training in the ADR (Alternative Dispute Resolution) field, you meet a lot of different people from different cultures. Since COVID, my customer base has widened, and I now work with people from Indonesia, Russia, India, Brazil, Italy, France, Ireland, the US, Rwanda and Japan, in addition to Norway – the opportunities have opened.

Before I started my company, I was inspired by the marketing strategy, *Blue Ocean Strategy: How to Create Uncontested Market Space and Make the Competition Irrelevant*. The ideas and steps from the *Blue Ocean Strategy* have helped me open training opportunities that I could not have imagined pre-COVID.

So, with participants from all these different countries, regions and continents, you might imagine how they have different approaches to negotiation styles, communication clarity, ethical awareness, and how precious or clear I must be in my instructions.

An amusing experience happened in St Petersburg when I told the participants they couldn't talk during an exercise. They could only show one of two letters as a signal on the screen, and I felt I had underscored quite well that this task only allowed them to talk later in the exercise.

The beauty of online training is that you can view all the participants' faces very well, but participants often forget how well they can be viewed. I suddenly saw several of them looking down below their table – you know, the way we used to cheat on tests back in Grade 7. I stopped the exercise and asked them what was happening. One embarrassed participant told me they had sent texts to each other during the exercise.

For me, this is a sweet story and one that confirms normal behaviour in negotiations – the willingness to win without an awareness of the effects your behaviour will have on the other party.

The mentality is to win at all costs, even in an exercise in negotiation training focusing on collaboration and how you build trust.

I believe this is much related to inherited mentality and the lack of awareness of what you are doing around the negotiation table or in front of the negotiation screen.

We were able to have a creative reflection time on perspectives and trust after this texting was stopped. I was also able to share a story from a training I attended at PON Harvard.

It happened on our first day of a week-long training, during a role-play with an elderly gentleman from the southern part of the US and a lawyer from a Mediterranean country. They made a deal in one of the role-plays, and during the reflection time they could not agree on the deal they had just made. After the discussion had waved back and forth, the Mediterranean man, who was joking and smiling said, 'I was just lying.' The southerner looked at him and said, 'I now know all I'll ever need to know about you for the rest of my life.' The Mediterranean responded, 'Come on! Calm down! I mean, this is only a game ... If you're going to get all upset because of a game, you'll never survive in the real world.'

Then the southerner closed the debate when he replied, 'No, my friend. The point is this *is* only a game. And if you will lie for points in a silly game, God only knows what you'd do for real money.'

TELL US ABOUT THE CRAICS, CROCODILE TEARS AND STANDOUT MOMENTS FROM THE LAST FEW YEARS

I have two takeaways from COVID times. One is the innovation of a new negotiation training concept and the other is a quote from a participant in a mediation competition. They relate to one word – MIND.

Let me start with the remarkable moment when a brilliant Indian law student in a mediation competition said to me, 'This is a MIND game.'

His quote is taken from the reflection round when I was a judge and gave feedback to him and his team. I used our sparring session to focus on the student's performance and related this to the concept of 'Negotiating with the Brain in MIND'. I wanted them to be more aware of how to process and leverage the other party's emotions, and to gather information with reflection and questions, more than arguments, so they could better determine the interests of the other party. By doing so, I wanted them to be aware and use techniques on how they could steer the negotiation productively when the other party was not responsive, or responsive but angry, or emotional while answering their questions. It was after we had exemplified what they did, and how they could change those situations that he leaned back in his chair. It was a moment I want to characterise as either, 'I have no idea what we are doing here,' or, 'I finally understand what this is about.'

I was very happy when it was the latter. I later learned that this team had changed their whole strategy after our sparring session, and they won the competition. A precious moment for him and his team and a standout for me to see the effect of learning in a sparring session and reflection round in international competitions.

The second standout for me is the innovation of a negotiation training concept my colleague Jason Liem and I have developed, with 'Negotiations with the Brain in MIND'. We have found it challenging, near impossible, to teach anyone how to resolve a conflict. Instead, we wanted to help develop the negotiators' and mediators' skills and improve their awareness and self-confidence, so they know how to better navigate the conflict they are to solve.

With this concept, we wanted to help the negotiators and mediators develop a broad range of diverse ideas and techniques that may succeed, depending on inherently unpredictable conditions. We know, with awareness, skills, preparation, reflection and tools, they will have a much better chance to succeed in their upcoming negotiation and mediation.

We want to raise their awareness of negotiation and how our brain affects us – so they can reflect on what they are doing in preparation for the next negotiation.

Together with my wife we have founded an NGO, Sport4Understanding, after we have visited and helped in groundwork dialogue for understanding – working voluntarily for an American conflict resolution organisation, PeacePlayers. They work with kids from divided areas and use basketball to connect them. I have seen the challenges between people who have lived separated by walls for a long time, and the distance creates *uncertainty* and *mistrust*, two words we focus on a lot. A wall is a sign of human weakness and a lack of ability to communicate. Where all communication is limited or even stopped, it will become impossible to solve conflicts.

In any conflict, it is easy to withdraw from each other and stop communicating, the seeds of mistrust start to grow and we create in-groups and out-groups to be suspicious of 'the others'.

In all our training we start with a focus on what we all can do something about the ME – ourselves. It is about the inner challenge each of us has with uncertainty, self-doubt and overthinking. It's later about the WE – the interaction with the other part. It is about the outer challenge of employing awareness and new skills to succeed.

In this, we challenge the participants to explore difficult issues together. It's about learning about ourselves, challenging our assumptions and skills, discovering others' views, as well as supporting and coaching each other, because we are in this conflict or situation together, and it's about giving ourselves and others room to make mistakes – we make ourselves vulnerable, human, to create a change.

An example of a change I later read about in the book *The Human Factor* by Archie Brown, about the relationship between Gorbachev, Reagan and Thatcher at the end of the Cold War. Among many events and correspondents between them, it's written that Gorbachev wrote to Thatcher seeking her support for the Soviet decision to impose 'a unilateral moratorium on all nuclear explosions and getting the US to do the same'.

To impose change, I'm sure Gorbachev had many inner challenges with uncertainty, self-doubt and overthinking before he made the interaction with Reagan and Thatcher; the outer challenge of employing awareness and new skills from the old mindset of former Soviet leaders to succeed.

We want to work with the participants to examine questions such as how does brain functioning get us into conflict and disputes? Why do seemingly rational and logical solutions not always work in negotiations? And how can brain science become our trusted friend?

The work we have done has helped us become more aware and it has helped participants we have worked with to take an overview of the situation, the case, the problem and the people they sit down with. We support them to help their MIND see the BIG PICTURE – to zoom out on the situation, see it in full context, and then zoom in again to work on the problems with a different MIND set.

As negotiators and mediators, we constantly need to remind ourselves to take a step back and make an overview of what is happening – here and now.

LOOKING FORWARD, WHAT DO YOU THINK MIGHT BE SOME LASTING TRENDS OR INFLUENCES?

Almost everything we do is about people – I believe some lasting trends or influences will be related to how we are skilled in interacting with people. There are two key elements I want to elaborate on: first, 'humanity is the key!' and second, facilitative leadership.

It's been great to see and experience how much we have been

able to change and adapt to when COVID 'hit us', yet all the restrictions demanded us to continue our work, but in new formats and new ways.

I believe lasting trends will be how we, 'in a normal way', will be working differently; a virtual office as normal as a fully furnished office, equal presence at the office as from our home offices, and meetings conducted online as well as onsite. The one thing that hasn't changed, and never will, is the interaction between people.

Therefore, I believe a lasting trend and a key success factor in tomorrow's workforce is human skills. Leaders across all disciplines, if they are executives, HR professionals, lawyers or mediators, need to develop the capacity to rise above the crisis and provide safe ways forward. In addition to their key technical or core skills, I believe the most successful ones are good human beings who wisely use their human skills, because conflict didn't go away with COVID, it changed. In some areas it reduced, and in others it grew, with differences dividing families, workplaces, communities and countries.

I have been blessed with many knowledgeable and skilled trainers on my pathway to becoming a negotiator and mediator myself.

They have three things in common. Firstly, they are very skilled and at the top of their field of expertise. Secondly, I feel they are humble about what they know and what they still need to discover and learn. And thirdly, I feel they all are enthusiastic about people.

Someone who has had the largest influence on me personally, my business development and the basis of my philosophy, is the American negotiator, lawyer, sports agent and author, Ron Shapiro. I have adopted his philosophy as mine:

'Negotiation is a collaboration, an effort undertaken by two

parties who will often have to work with each other long after the deal is done.'

In today's polarised world, we risk losing the human 'touch' that formed the basis for many negotiations. All too often, so-called icons in the business world, and certainly in the political world, appear as successful and known for their harsh approach, for crushing their opponents and leaving them with nothing. I believe this method, more times than not, does not work in the long run. I believe 'humanity is the key!'

In Wægger Negotiation Institute's work, we facilitate. The goal of facilitating leadership is to empower our participants and clients to make decisions and to promote better communication and productivity in the group. Parties in mediation often experience the situation as chaotic and unfocused.

In such situations and many others, facilitating leadership can be of good use. It is a suitable tool that allows the parties, participants or sparring partners to make decisions, handle disagreements or conflicts and take responsibility for challenges. It is a proprietary tool because it is an effective way to lead creative processes among high-performing participants.

In the book, *Good for You, Great for Me*, Professor Lawrence Susskind, describes facilitation:

'Facilitation can be viewed as a bundle of meeting-management skills that anyone can employ, such as coordinating the flow of conversation, ensuring that participants observe time limits, cooling tempers when talks get overheated, and periodically summarizing the essence of working agreements.'

I believe a developing trend will be related to interacting with people in different organisational structures. I believe we will develop more flattened organisations with facilitative leaders, with skills such as how to ask good questions and engaging listening. Leaders with problem-solving skills to create value. Leaders who foster empowerment in their co-workers to make winning at win-win negotiations a reality.

Leaders of tomorrow will need to take more responsibility, and companies need to find and develop leaders who can motivate, define what needs to be done, take initiative and responsibility and encourage collaborations.

Facilitative leadership is a trend I would like to see more of in the future; leaders who consult with the people they are leading, who support and advise existing ideas to develop into meaningful new ideas, and leaders who have the skills and ability to work with their staff to reach their common goal.

YOUR TIPS FOR DEALING WITH PEOPLE DYNAMICS DURING CONFUSION, CHANGE AND CONFLICT

Being a facilitator is about connecting people with each other, addressing the problems they're struggling with and helping them create opportunities for the future.

My first tip is to be present in all you do. Presence, for me, is a key characteristic of a facilitating leadership style, and it helps time after time to accept and emphasise diversity and authenticity, meaning that conflict resolution is not only written in an agreement, but the conflict or disagreement is resolved in such a way that the agreement is implemented.

The second and third tips are additional characteristics of facilitation, and I encourage you to use them in your upcoming negotiation or leadership.

One of these characteristics is to be able to give direction without taking control. I suggest attempting to facilitate so participants reflect more than they react. It's challenging, but it's imperative to ensure engaged listening so that all voices are heard.

Another characteristic is to balance the management of both the content and the processes within the group. Having the awareness of the process on how a group acts is critical to success and deserves considerable attention.

This is not about avoiding conflict, but rather seeing the positive side of the conflict, encouraging open, honest and respectful dialogue. All voices need to be heard, developed, challenged and evaluated.

This can often be difficult because we all intuitively evaluate our initial assumptions in a way that builds on our experiences. You can try imagining how your decision would be made and what might go wrong. In my training, I say to the participants preparing for a simulation case, 'Be aware of your biases but question them. Make assumptions, but don't react to them – question them, and develop many questions for other parties.'

When working with others in negotiations, and when conflicts arise, it is a major challenge, because often the person and the problem become one. We can start to view the other as an object, not a person, and that's when it's most important to remember 'humanity is the key!'

BIO

Roar felt so passionately about negotiation and mediation that he decided to leave his work as a lawyer in the traditional legal industry and founded Wægger Negotiation Institute in 2017. He is a Harvard PON's and Pepperdine Straus Institute's trained negotiator, mediator and conflict resolution specialist. He is also a Singapore International Mediation Institute (SIMI) Accredited Civil/Commercial Mediator, a certified UK civil/commercial mediator, and a certified mediator by the Norwegian Bar Association.

He now helps organisations build effective negotiating expertise and cultures that will enable them to better raise revenue and build strong business relationships. This is his passion and is what gives him energy for the next day at work. By guiding and training individuals and teams in negotiation and conflict management, he can positively impact the business and optimise activity. Roar's goal is to limit his clients' time and the harrowing emotional strains of long conflict processes, or at worst, costly litigation. His experience has taught him that problem-solving and effective negotiations through systematic preparation produce better results.

wni.as/en/home/

SAM HARDY
BOUNCING FORWARD NOT BACK

I wonder if we should use the opportunity to reset.
Rather than bouncing back, let's bounce forward.

PUSH TO RESET

As we move into a stage of 'trying to get back to normal' I wonder if we should use the opportunity to reset. Rather than bouncing back, let's bounce forward, and not necessarily go back to what we had.

TELL US ABOUT WHAT YOU DO AND WHAT YOU LOVE ABOUT IT

I call myself a 'PRACADEMIC' – a mixture of practitioner and academic. I run a conflict management practice (including conflict management coaching, mediation and related services) and I conduct academic work (teaching in universities, corporate training and research). I also run a conflict leadership program for a select group of international leaders and practitioners who meet regularly via Zoom for coaching, training, reflective practice, inter-vision and peer support.

Mostly what I focus on these days is conflict management coaching, as well as providing professional development training for leaders and coaches from all over the world to increase their conflict management skills towards artistry. I really enjoy teaching and helping people to increase their competence and confidence to manage and resolve conflict. I train people from many different contexts all over the world. I am currently running two corporate training programs for government agencies in Australia and the US. I also have a number of online courses that people can do as individuals.

Working in this environment combines two things I really like: helping people and getting to know what makes them 'tick'. I'm curious about people and intrigued and fascinated by the fact that we sometimes (frequently) work against ourselves. And conflict is an area where that happens a lot! I like to help people work with and for themselves, and to be their best selves in difficult times.

TELL US A LITTLE ABOUT HOW COVID IMPACTED WHAT YOU DO AND HOW YOU ADAPTED

This may sound a little harsh, given how much suffering so many people went through, but luckily for me, I already had a head-start on working in an online environment. With clients all over the world and travel difficult with a young daughter with serious medical issues, I was already transitioning to working predominantly online, so for me it wasn't too much of a pivot.

Prior to COVID I had already begun developing online courses and experimenting with platforms like Zoom, so while many of my colleagues were scrambling to replace their live training programs, for me, the timing seemed right and I was already doing things asynchronously with a good understanding of the technology. I found I had already experimented with getting the best quality internet connection and the technology to support it. The hardest thing for me was managing time zones; it was often a bit of a nightmare. I can't count how many times I was early, or worse, late, for something I'd scheduled.

I soon discovered that my assumption that face-to-face was always better wasn't necessarily the case, though I did have to adapt to a slightly different mindset when working consistently online. I think working in a comfortable zone, sitting on a couch, wearing your Ugg boots if you wanted to, was a bonus! Another pleasant change I noticed over this period was that people learnt to be a bit more flexible and forgiving. We were all in the same situation, working from home, often sick, sometimes with kids also in isolation with us. Everyone developed an understanding that 'things happened' and sometimes someone was running late or had to change their plans at the last minute. It took away a lot of pressure when things didn't go to plan because everyone was going through it. Compassion for one another has been a really interesting by-product from the experience, and I hope we don't lose that essence.

Now, out of isolation, it's created a little conflict around things like vaccinations and debates about returning to the office on a more regular basis, as well as simply adapting back into face-to-face environments. Brené Brown has a great term to describe the transition back into the office – 'the great awkward'. I truly believe that there is still a strong element of compassion, understanding and acknowledgement of flexibility. I guess it's about keeping everything in balance.

TELL US ABOUT DEALING WITH CONFUSION, CHANGE AND CONFLICT SINCE WE'VE BEEN IMPACTED BY COVID

I put a lot of thought into how confusion and change have made an impact, and when I started to write down a few notes, I ended up with a 'huge' list. There were so many thoughts, it seemed easier to put it into a bullet-point list – disclaimer: these are just *my thoughts* on the impact COVID has had on all of us.
- People are under increased stress. This sees their resilience and capacity for change decrease. Little things seem harder to deal with and the emotions can be less regulated.
- People have different priorities. People now look at things with a different perspective, and in some cases, this allowed them to let go of conflict through their new perspective.
- People experience heightened emotions adding to the pressures of victimhood. In conflict this will often lead people to see themselves as passive helpless victims, and that is reinforced by the uncertainties and challenges associated with COVID. It's a complex situation which can lead to making it harder

for people to make smart choices and engage in a constructive way.
- People feel they have less control over their lives. This leads to them being more rigid in the things they think they can control. Victimhood itself can sometimes be a thing that can be controlled, as a way to manipulate or even avoid accountability. This then has impact on conflict. When we're feeling resilient, we will nip conflict in the bud much quicker, being more likely to have a direct conversation. But when feeling like a victim, that conflict is not dealt with in a constructive way and is often left to simmer and fester, having a greater impact on our mental health.
- People will respond to turbulent times in very different ways at different times. *We may be in the same storm, but we're not all in the same boat.* With a sustained issue like COVID, we tend to experience ebbs and flows. At times we will be even more resilient in difficult times, and that's when we need to notice that feeling and take positive action or make changes. When we are not feeling as strong, it's okay to have some self-compassion and give ourselves a break and not make difficult decisions during that time. It's not all or nothing. With some self-reflection we can recognise those moments, and adapt our level of engagement to fit the ebbs and flows.
- People may be generally overwhelmed, with more uncertainty and doubt. During this time, people may only be capable of short-term thinking, no longer able to see the bigger picture. Their confidence is low and choices are focused on 'right now' and not how that may impact their future.
- People may disengage as a self-care strategy – and that may be a smart choice in the moment for their mental and physical health. It doesn't necessarily mean they are going to disengage

forever. It can be a sensible self-care strategy to give yourself permission to rebuild yourself to a healthy state after a couple of years of carrying anxieties and lowered resilience.
- People may downplay or feel guilty about their suffering compared with others. Some of us might not express our needs or challenges because it just doesn't seem that bad, after what others have been through. 'I mean, I can complain about the weather but I'm not experiencing floods like the people in Lismore.' However, it's never useful to compare yourself to others and it's important to ask for help if you validly need it. Comparing your circumstances to others can discourage you from seeking support.

Sometimes in conflict, the certainty of what we have now, even if it's objectively unpleasant, feels better than the uncertainty of taking a step and trying to do something different. In uncertain times, like COVID, we cling on to any certainty that we think we have control over. It doesn't make sense objectively, but it feels safer to stick with what you know, even if it sucks.

As we move into a stage of 'trying to get back to normal' I wonder if we should use the opportunity to reset. Rather than bouncing back, let's bounce forward, and not necessarily go back to what we had. What can we change or improve? Can we bounce forward into something better?

TELL US ABOUT THE CRAICS, CROCODILE TEARS AND STANDOUT MOMENTS FROM THE LAST FEW YEARS

One silly example was when I was doing a pre-mediation session and my dog pooped on the carpet behind me, in full view of the video. I don't know why because he would never normally do that. He's supposed to be toilet trained … it was awkward! At least technology doesn't transmit smells (yet)! Then there are the moments when children run across the room half-naked or bring you things to look at during some very significant times in the negotiations … (Three year old: 'Hey, Mum, I caught this for you!' Me: 'Ummm, is that a poo?!') There's definitely a theme here, I've realised!

I have seen some really difficult situations in which people's livelihoods were destroyed and communities divided as a direct result of COVID. Like the remote medical centre that only had two nurses. They each worked twelve-hour shifts to manage an entire region, but were often required to work up to twenty hours just to service the area. When compulsory vaccinations were introduced, one nurse refused to be vaccinated, and so she wasn't allowed to work. The nurse who was vaccinated was then required to cover the entire twenty-four-hour shift. So, it had a very significant effect on her that went far beyond their disagreement about whether or not they should be vaccinated. In very small communities, some of those impacts were much more significant and challenging for people to manage. It becomes really personal if people require medical care and the nurse is exhausted or she's not there because she's gone for a meal. They're blaming her, which is unfair. And then the nurse who hadn't been vaccinated was ostracised by the community, and her family suffered by association. I think situations like these often went a little bit under the radar because they weren't big things that got into the news. But it is these 'small' conflicts that have big ripple effects, and there isn't any easy or logical way to manage them.

The things that brought me joy were the situations in which some of the challenges actually led clients to go back to their values and face the hard questions about what they really wanted for their future. Many clients were able to discover their 'true north' through their adversity. This kind of learning, resilience and growth through suffering is one of the things that I think reminds us that humans have infinite potential, in good times and in bad.

SHARE YOUR HACKS, INNOVATIONS OR LEARNINGS THAT HAVE EMERGED FROM THIS TIME

Often in conflict, we want to repair things, to get things back to the way they were before the conflict. For me, I would recommend that instead of asking how we can get 'back' to the way things were, try asking, 'How can we improve?' How can we develop and how can we grow? Viktor Frankl talks about learning from suffering, and I think this is the attitude we can encourage. How can we learn from this challenge? I don't mean that we should discount people's suffering with toxic positivity ('Just keep calm and carry on, it could be worse!'), but acknowledge and learn from the experience.

If nothing else over this time, we realised that we could do things differently because we had to. It doesn't necessarily mean we found the 'best way' but we found a way to move forward, and there is still room to move from here.

I also discovered that we can participate in difficult conversations, mediations and coaching sessions in a virtual environment, and this had some surprising benefits. For example, we didn't have to rush to be somewhere, fight peak-hour traffic or have a conversation in an unfamiliar room. I had previously devalued working online compared to face to face, but I found that being in our own space helped people to be more regulated and less anxious than if we'd connected in a strange room. I also found that it was not any more difficult to recognise others' emotions in a video conference compared to face to face. While we may not be able to see as much body language, it's surprising how much we can notice from facial expression and tone of voice.

One hack when working online is to be up on your technology and have good backup plans in place in case something goes wrong. A few times I've had situations when someone's wi-fi was a really bad connection or the power went out in the middle of the session. My conflict leadership group and I came up with a checklist of things to consider before going online, including having the contact details of a neighbour or someone else in the house should it be impossible to get in contact with a participant. There are also important considerations to ensure participants' safety and wellbeing when you are not physically in the room with them, and they may be in an entirely different location. You need to have emergency numbers and referral pathways for support services that are in the clients' locations, as your own local ones may be too far away.

I love the asynchronous opportunities for learning in the online environment. While I love having everyone in the room at the same time, this is not always convenient for people if they have caring responsibilities or work different hours. Having asynchronous online courses opens up learning opportunities for people who might otherwise not be able to attend a face-to-face workshop. It also allows conversations to take place between people from different parts of the world, which adds diversity to the discussion.

LOOKING FORWARD, WHAT DO YOU THINK MIGHT BE SOME LASTING TRENDS OR INFLUENCES?

I think there are two distinct groups, not just in our industry, but in all industries. There's the 'return to business as usual' community, who are looking to return to the 'good old days and ways'. Then there are the people who are adapting, growing and innovating with hybrid ways of doing things. I believe the hybrid way of doing things is the way forward, and these are the people who will thrive.

I think we will continue to use technology and we'll combine it with our standard face-to-face interactions. I don't think that technology should ever be a replacement, but it's a nice complement to it. It allows us to reach different people, to be more inclusive, in many ways. People have different abilities, different travel possibilities, different time zones, different care commitments, so I think the hybrid approach is a good thing. There's a flexibility and a willingness to accommodate different people's needs to interact in different ways. We used to talk about different learning styles and we'd say some people are visual, some people are auditory. I think what COVID has done has helped us incorporate that into our practice, not just our teaching, but our practice, adapting to different people's ways of communicating and what people feel comfortable with. There may be different styles for different purposes. Having plenty of choices, gives everyone a chance to interact in a way that works best for them.

YOUR TIPS FOR DEALING WITH PEOPLE DYNAMICS DURING CONFUSION, CHANGE AND CONFLICT

- Take the time to assess people's capacity for conflict resolution (this is similar to a risk assessment but not quite the same thing). Spend more time in intake conversations to check a person's level of resilience and emotional regulation. This is particularly important if you are working with people online,

because if something goes wrong online, it's much harder to offer support in the moment.
- In turbulent times, check if the work can be structured into smaller, more manageable interventions. Help people to develop achievable goals and scaffold their action planning to help build their resilience and confidence. Any small positive achievement is a step towards the end goal. Ensure that wherever possible you give others some certainty, even if it's only certainty about the process and the next few steps.
- Consider whether conflict management processes or interventions can happen concurrently when someone is managing other challenges. Sometimes it can be more beneficial to put things on hold until life is a bit more stable and everyone is feeling more resilient and able to engage confidently.

Ultimately, I think COVID was the catalyst for a lot of us to take a good hard look at ourselves and how we respond in challenging and turbulent times. In many parts of the world people go through turbulent times like war and famine on a fairly regular basis, and COVID was a reminder to those of us who had become complacent that we're not isolated from life's challenges. Whether it's worldwide, countrywide or a personal crisis for ourselves or one of our clients, friends or family, those waves are always going to be there, and we're going to get dumped at some point. All we can do is be as prepared as we possibly can for the storms that come. The recent global challenges have been a prompt for reflection, learning and growth, so we can develop the confidence to bounce forward and not bounce back. That's been my moral over the past few years.

My main message is to look after yourself first ('fit your own oxygen mask before attempting to help others'). Only then can you support others effectively, in whichever role or capacity that may be. It's not always easy, but I am consciously aware that I need to be at my best so I can support others to be at their best.

BIO

Samantha Hardy provides coaching and training in conflict management and resolution. She practices primarily in the workplace context and in the university sector. Sam has been accredited as a mediator under the Australian National Mediation System and is a Certified Transformative Mediator by the US Institute of Conflict Transformation. She is a certified narrative coach practitioner, an experienced conflict coach and the founder of the REAL Conflict Coaching System. She holds a PhD in law and conflict resolution, as well as other postgraduate qualifications in education. Sam is also a well-known university educator, holding adjunct professorial appointments in Australia, Singapore, Hong Kong and the USA. She has also published widely in conflict resolution and her online courses are leading the way to help practitioners better understand the impact of emotions on conflict and its resolution.

Sam's passion and mission is to make conflict no longer a dirty word. To help people develop their skills and confidence to manage conflict well so that they can create a peaceful future in all aspects of their lives.

samanthahardy.com.au

SHANTI ABRAHAM MATHEW
POLLINATING OUR MEDIATION LANDSCAPE

Mediation is just one part of a broader ecosystem, and our role as mediators is to pollinate the landscape with potential for resolution, problem-solving and peace.

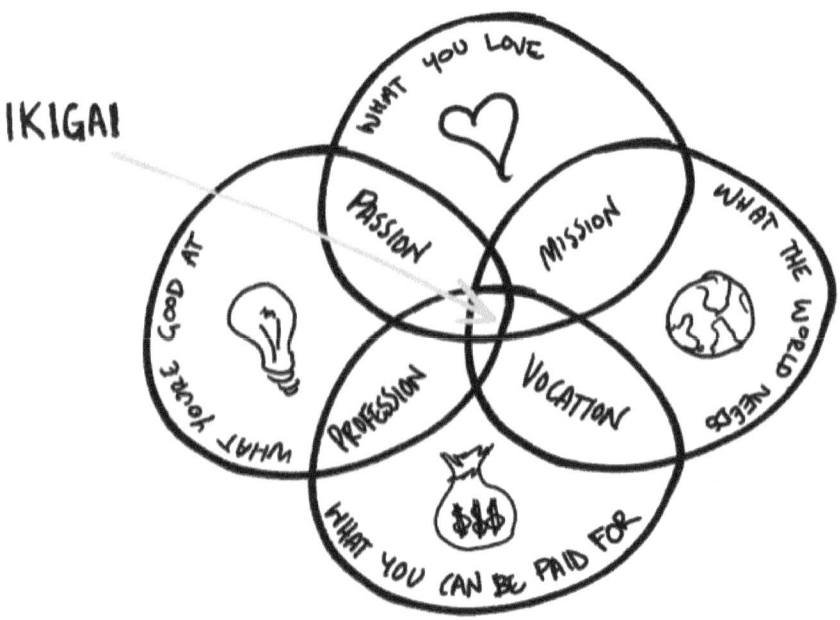

Have you ever heard the term *ikigai*? It's a Japanese concept that means your reason for being. In Japanese 'life' and 'gai' describes your value or worth. Your ikigai is your life purpose.

TELL US ABOUT WHAT YOU DO AND WHAT YOU LOVE ABOUT WHAT YOU DO

Originally from Singapore, I'm now in Kuala Lumpur and have been living and working in Malaysia for the last twenty-five years. I'm an advocate, solicitor, corporate lawyer, arbitrator and adjudicator, but my favourite hat of all is as a mediator. I've been in practice for twenty-seven years now and my range of work and experience has been quite eclectic. I started off doing litigation in construction work and moved on to corporate work including contract drafting, mergers and acquisitions and infrastructure work including the sale of a port in Myanmar. With all that corporate experience, mediation was not too difficult a shift in my workflow, because at the negotiation table, there's no such thing as 'winning', rather the deal has to be done. It is not about who is the smartest or loudest person at the table, it's about everyone around the table being smart enough to get the deal done.

I was introduced to mediation through my husband, a senior maritime lawyer, who was among the first lawyers in Malaysia to be trained by Australian mediation trainers. He came home after the gruelling training, and he said, 'You know, I think you'll be good at this.' Though I had never heard of mediation before, once I put my toe in the water a few years later, mediation and the facilitative mediation process seemed to answer so many questions I had about effective problem-solving.

Have you ever heard the term *ikigai*? It's a Japanese concept that means your reason for being. In Japanese 'life' and 'gai' describes your value or worth. Your ikigai is your life purpose. I love the work of doing mediation and being part of understanding the nuances of a problem and structuring solutions. I love the work of teaching mediation, and now mediation advocacy is my big thing. Mediation advocacy has been an area that has been under-served, under-respected and under-trained until now.

TELL US A LITTLE ABOUT HOW COVID IMPACTED WHAT YOU DO AND HOW YOU ADAPTED

When COVID started, I was in my twenty-fifth year of practice. My firm had been planning on having a party to celebrate me being a lawyer for a quarter of a century. Then COVID hit. The hard reality was that we were at the beginning of the year and cashflow was an issue. I had just completed a matrimonial mediation, where the parties had impressive assets including flashy cars, but no cash to pay for the mediation. We were waiting for the money from that mediation to pay bills, and I was having to grapple with the idea of what COVID might mean to me. Was practice as I knew it coming to an end? I also realised that so many people in disputes would be in awful positions. They would also be having a cashflow crisis and wondering what to do. That is when I wondered whether it was time for mediation to mainstream and move forward in Malaysia. I dared to dream outside the 'box' so I came up with an idea to try to persuade the Malaysian government to create a world-first and provide funding to foot the bill for mediation services for the Malaysian public.

We wanted to try and mediate matters which, because of COVID, couldn't go to court, couldn't go for arbitration or any of the formal processes. We were already signatories to the Singapore Convention, and although it had absolutely nothing to do with the Malaysian COVID-19 Mediation Legislation, I think the project helped to plant the idea that mediation could provide some solutions. I was clear that lawyers had to be a part of this problem-solving system, because the moment you exclude the lawyers, they're just going to oppose whatever the system is which they perceive to be a threat to their rice bowl. So that was my challenge. But I'm so proud of this program and how everyone worked to make it happen. The Malaysia's COVID-19 Mediation Centre is a world-first that benefited both the community and the community of mediators, because the government pays the mediator, not a token payment, but a decent sum of money that reflects that the government values what they do.

The program was meant to be for one year and was extended to two years. It was hard, because people didn't really understand what mediation was, and again, we needed to create the links with the lawyers. What we recognised during COVID was our frontline workers and health care professionals carried a heavy load. There was also an emerging secondary cost. In recognising the disputes, financial costs and problems that were emerging, we created a new phrase called 'NEXTLINERS'. We recognised the fallout from COVID-related problems would translate into disputes. We needed lawyers onboard, working with mediators to help solve these emerging problems. At this point the government said, 'Okay, we'll include the lawyers and that is when there was a push for the 'Mediate First' policy for law firms. Whilst we have a long way to go, we do have fifty-five law firms who have engaged and given a pledge to Mediate First for COVID-related disputes. We are hopeful that this is a conversation that will continue and who knows what the next version will be, perhaps Mediation Centre 2.0!

TELL US ABOUT DEALING WITH CONFUSION, CHANGE AND CONFLICT SINCE WE'VE BEEN IMPACTED BY COVID

I don't think I've seen a huge change. Usually, people will be motivated by the outcomes they perceive they are going to get.

However, while we were in the epicentre of COVID, I saw tremendous change in the conversation. I had people calling me up saying, 'Shanti, we have an arbitration clause, no mediation clause, but can the parties come for mediation?' People didn't want to just sit and swelter in their problems, they wanted solutions. You would think after all those kinds of inquiries that the cases for mediation would increase, but a lot of them ended up going straight to resolution because everyone was just overwhelmed with their different problems. They wanted to unlock cash as quickly as possible. I remember a situation where I had nine inquiries in one week and zero converted to mediation. I'm sure everyone had this because, it was just people reaching out.

I also had expatriate parents calling me to say, 'I've been deprived of access to my child, can we mediate this? Can we do it on Zoom?' It was a real education for all of us. I admit, I was not a believer in online meetings, but I am now. What we are seeing now though is people going back to face-to-face mediations, as people feel comfortable with this type of interaction. But for cross-border work, online works well.

Traditionally, when people find themselves in conflict, when things are heated and when they are angry, their bias usually points them toward the biggest, loudest and most aggressive lawyer in town. They litigate and go to court because everyone goes in wanting to win. For the professional, it's part of the fun with the hoped outcome of winning and 'being right!' But parties don't often realise that litigation can be like stepping onto the badminton court – they (the parties) are the shuttlecock that gets whacked around, while the lawyers are holding the badminton racquet enjoying the game and invariably improving their skills and agility on the court again and again. There's nothing wrong with being a badminton racquet holder or even to enjoy the thrill of the game, because that's what you do on a badminton court.

Unfortunately, many people don't realise, until it's too late, that this usually only leads to one outcome. A winner. A loser. A used-up shuttlecock.

I am very happy to say that in the last two to three years, I have observed an increase in non-lawyer consultants using the language of mediation and referring disputes to mediators. I've had work referred to me by accountants, architects and business consultants, and have been regularly put forward as a mediator or mediation advocate. They seem to have captured the idea of solving matters quickly, likely because that's their deliverable. In one case, an associate I've known for sixteen years spoke to a gentleman, asking, 'Why are you are stretching out the conflict? Why don't you try mediation first?' There had been a perception on his part that mediation didn't or couldn't work for 'large' dispute resolutions. Thankfully, that is changing.

TELL US ABOUT THE CRAICS, CROCODILE TEARS AND STANDOUT MOMENTS FROM THE LAST FEW YEARS

When I reflect on the past few years there are little glimpses of standout moments. The fact that mediation for COVID-related matters became part of the Malaysian COVID-19 Act was a very touching moment for me. Even though, in itself, mediation is brilliant, there hasn't been one standout moment as there have been so many little but significant ones. I recently contributed to a book on negotiation, mediation and settlement, and it was interesting, because in the conversations I had preceding that request, they said, 'We're not sure who to talk to about mediation,' and it was a little sobering. I've been talking about mediation for more than ten years (others have for more than twenty years in

Malaysia) and whilst it is wonderful to be involved in their book, it makes me realise we have a long way to go in how we advocate for mediation. Part of the challenge is that we don't have a lot of BIG success stories we can share.

I was sharing with someone recently about a mediation that I had helped to resolve. It was a high multi-million-dollar case. It initially came to me as an arbitration, but the party did not realise how expensive arbitration was going to be for a multi-million-dollar matter. He originally came to see me because they thought they would appoint me as the mediator, but then there's a point in the conversation where they've shared too much. For me, I reached that point and just said, 'I think I'll be more useful to you as your mediation advocate.' He wasn't sure about that as he thought he needed a 'barracuda'. I told him that, 'On a bad day I can be the barracuda, but at all other times, I am a problem-solver.' What helped turn him to agree to this was that I did the comparison table of the mediation costs versus the arbitration costs and showed him there was plenty of room to negotiate. He decided he was going to do it, and a year later, I felt that mixed emotion of elation at resolving a matter and the anticlimactic freeze moment of realising a meal ticket had come to a close. We might as well be honest about these conflicting emotions. We worked really hard to get to a resolution and we finally resolved the matter. My client could never have imagined that we would have settled, and I must have faith that more paid work is coming up the pipe. Now I have a story that I can share; a story that shows that mediation can work in big commercial matters. As I write this, that client has now steered another friend in litigation in my direction, telling his friend to strongly seek my counsel. It is heartwarming that the mediative efforts made an impact.

SHARE YOUR HACKS, INNOVATIONS OR LEARNINGS THAT HAVE EMERGED FROM THIS TIME

Persistence is the rule of the game. The biggest problem for successful mediations is the counterparty, because depending on their choice of advisor, you can clearly see the trajectory of whether you're going to hit a wall or impasse quite early in the journey.

I've had incredible pessimists in the room. They would be tantamount to being the 'spanner in the works'.

I've trained myself not to react to them – instead, I respond.

For example, there are senior lawyers who want to make a gender statement. More than a few times, I've heard the comment, 'You must have such a supportive husband.' In a nod towards the apparently unlucrative aspect of mediation. I don't react and instead focus on the problem-solving.

I need to trust that persistence will get us to the finish line. It is hard work, but when you keep persevering, you keep moving towards that point where a mediation practice is sustainable.

I am privileged that I am able to share my success stories as well as the challenging ones. It is powerful when you can share your stories of mediation. Even when they fail, your ability to persist and to push forward for a solution provides such great learning for everyone else who finds themselves in conflict.

The Singapore International Mediation Centre recently shared one of their stories, and it highlights how mediators aren't just doing 'small value' mediations; this was a big case. The article shares the first failed attempt and how they pushed towards the finishing line. That's what I love about the story; it doesn't matter that it was messy and complicated.

And finally, one of my key learnings has been the power of unshakable belief that mediation can solve a vast majority of issues and conflicts.

I'm not Pollyanna, and I realise there will always be some issues of law, but that's where my experience as a litigator and as an arbitration counsel comes in very helpful.

All my previous experience and skills come back to assist the client, but it's my clarity on my purpose, my 'ikigai', that drives me forward. If you want to fight a battle, you need warriors, but when you want to solve a problem, you need to get a problem-solving lawyer, which is special KIND of WARRIOR, into the picture. Often it's the mediation advocate who is also a mediator who bring this to the table. We can't all wait around for appointments – we need to be case creators as well.

It's such a powerful moment when it all becomes apparent and everyone realises that most of issues can be resolved. And while most of us in this field are the optimists, we must, in some ways, respect the pessimist. To embrace that pessimism but persevere anyway. This is what will help us help them create practical and sustainable outcomes.

LOOKING FORWARD, WHAT DO YOU THINK MIGHT BE SOME LASTING TRENDS OR INFLUENCES?

With legal practitioners, there are often competing demands to ensure that their legal practice is sustainable, and therefore billing targets are prioritised over outcomes. This creates a culture of litigation, with very few involved thinking in terms of resolving the problem quickly and giving the client the smallest bill possible.

That is the business of 'lawyering' and that's how lawyers operate. That's why I'm sympathetic when I talk to senior lawyers, because mediation is a complete shift in their frame of reference. It's a complete shift to their whole business model. For the last eight years here in Malaysia, we've been talking about this business model, because unless mediation work is sustainable and lawyers can make a living, put their children through university and prepare for retirement, mediation as we know it is not going to take off.

When I first went to Harvard in 2014, I decided to put this idea into a business model of practice. It was not an easy decision, and I couldn't have done it without the support of my husband, the litigator. The first thing I did was say, 'We're not paying ourselves enough.' We were not acknowledging how clever this process is, and that it must be rewarded. If it's not rewarded, then it is a practice for the rich, the retired and the bored, which to be honest, is still mostly the demographic of many mediators (i.e. a job they do AFTER they have put their kids through university and saved for their own retirement). Even the mediation believers did not see that they had a role in pollinating the landscape, and in doing so, the landscape was barren, with very few cases, and the occasional few flowers that people got to pick.

I'm still quite troubled by the fact that it's not yet a sustainable profession. What will keep the mediation drum beating is the right economics. If we are mediation advocates first, and mediators second, we understand and can convey the economics of doing mediation, while maintaining the respect, value and sustainability of mediation. In doing so, we will create a landscape where you and I will be able to send our children to university on a mediator's income. During a mediation, I once openly said to a lawyer on the other side, 'You know, this file will send my kids to university, and I have twins!' We all laughed. It was one of those moments where everybody in the room wanted to resolve the issue. I love it when both sides' clients realise they've got the good guys in the room. And we're not soft, we're 100% facts; firm on policies and firm on durability. I am not designing agreements that are going to fall apart. I build in mediation clauses to contracts.

What we need is a few success stories where the stakeholders come back together again. We mustn't sell the advisors short. We need to be talking up what we do, or we may end up shooting ourselves in the foot. When a lawyer suggests to their client to go to mediation, the clients will often think that the lawyers can be both lawyer and mediator, but often when a lawyer puts on a mediator's hat, it is not good for our industry. It makes things harder. The issue usually turns into a negotiation with mediative principles. That is why the role of the mediation advocate is so important; we are pollinating the field of dispute resolution, planting the seeds for the future of our mediation industry. With more and more people being trained in mediation, over the last year or so, it's important for everyone in the legal industry, and ourselves, to value what we do.

YOUR TIPS FOR DEALING WITH PEOPLE DYNAMICS DURING CONFUSION, CHANGE AND CONFLICT

- Invest in your life, not in your disputes. Focus on your business, and how you can get out of any disputes as quickly as possible. Choose to invest in your life, moving forward rather than investing in the dispute.
- If you find yourself in conflict, if you are in the centre of a storm, get a sensible person to help you. Find the RIGHT advisor, someone who is a problem-solver.
- Get clear on what you are working towards – the biggest barracuda in town is unlikely to help you mediate a solution,

they might win the battle but often the cost is high. When you get clarity about what matters to you, you can make better decisions.
- Be real about problem-solving and be prepared to listen. At the beginning of a conflict there is lots of anger, and in this anger, people are less likely to listen. They call in the barracuda to have the fight, thinking mediation is soft and fluffy and ineffective. The one thing they aren't prepared to do is listen.
- At some point, a choice is required, *Am I prepared to live like this, or am I ready to resolve the problem?* You need to solve those conflict problems, otherwise you carry those problems with you going forward.

BIO

Shanti brings over twenty-five years of legal experience in both Malaysia and Singapore to her own boutique legal practice, Messrs Shanti Abraham & Associates in Kuala Lumpur, and has practiced as an advocate and solicitor in both Singapore and Kuala Lumpur. As a mediator, Shanti is SIMI Certified Mediator and a Principal Mediator with the Singapore Mediation Centre. She is also a mediator with the Malaysian Mediation Centre. Having attended several Harvard negotiation courses, she is now a trainer across the region and enjoys the innovation that mediation brings to problem-solving in the legal context. Shanti is also a mediator of the Global Mediation Panel at the Office of the Ombudsman for UN Funds and Programs. She was appointed as a health care mediator on the specialist panel of the Singapore Mediation Centre as well as to SIDREC (Securities Industries Dispute Resolution Centre) where she mediates and adjudicates regularly. Shanti has mediated over one hundred cases (including family mediations) today with more than eighty cases logged and more than twenty feedback forms from willing parties. Her success rate over the last ten years is more than 80% of matters resolved. Shanti can handle multi-party mediations with complexity and cross-border parties. She has been trained in mediation process design at the Advance Mediation Programme at Harvard Law School.

Shanti actively advocates appropriate solutions in problem-solving. The many available solutions include neutral evaluation, expert determination, mediation, arbitration as well as litigation. Shanti is prepared to advise on the most sensible and cost-effective approach a client requires to address their concerns and continues to have a mixed practice of civil litigation and corporate work.

shantiabraham.com

SREE SWAMINATHAN
ADAPTABILITY IS THE KEY TO SUCCESS

Negotiation happens in many ways in our day-to-day life, and I can't stress this enough, listening is key. We all have had to learn to negotiate around complex issues at work and in our communities, but in anything and everything, listening and having your ears open all the time is an absolute necessity.

Being an IT company, cybersecurity is a core focus for us, and it started with us making sure our own business was secure; 'look at your own house, before you say anything about others'. We've had to ensure that we frequently visit our own technical environment, as this is key, hackers come up with absolutely brilliant ways of thinking and operating.

TELL US ABOUT WHAT YOU DO AND WHAT YOU LOVE ABOUT WHAT YOU DO

I am CEO in the technology industry, and with my partner, operate six IT and telecommunication companies across Australia. Our head office is based in Melbourne and our main focus is medium-to-large enterprises. I started my first business when I was sixteen years old in India, with my brother who is three years older than me. It was an IT company and HR firm with a lean towards the recruitment side of business. This business has now got branches in Dubai and the US, so the baby has grown bigger, which is fantastic. When I was twenty-one, I moved to Australia, and started working with a finance company, working my way from the bottom up. I also completed my masters in finance and started the business here in Australia. I now have staff all over the world, including in the Philippines, India, Melbourne, Queensland and Perth. We have a great relationship with our clients and that is how we have grown. Our core value is trust in everything and anything we do.

I am passionate about making sure clients are satisfied and showing them what more we can do for them and for their business. In doing so, we grow as well. It's like growing together, journeying side by side. Many of our clients have travelled with us for up to sixteen years. They have started as a one-person business and have now grown into multi-billion-dollar businesses. For me, the passion is more of helping clients. I love the adrenaline of a challenge, facing the challenges and solving them to the best of my ability is something I cherish. I also love that along the way, you can watch the employees grow. They become like family, watching them get married, having kids, meeting their family, telling them about how well they are doing with us. It's just the sheer joy of family combined with a professional environment.

TELL US A LITTLE ABOUT HOW COVID IMPACTED WHAT YOU DO AND HOW YOU ADAPTED

Our main headquarters is based in Melbourne, so we have had to deal and with some very big differences in how our business was operating in Melbourne, as compared to Perth and some other states. Melbourne experienced one of the longest lockdowns in the world, so we had a massive hit. We were unable to travel between the states and support our business nationally, and this did put a big dent in terms of the profitability and on how we managed our staff in different locations. In Melbourne, many of the staff were working from home, sales did go down, but we focused on our core principle of helping to keep businesses running. I'm proud to say that we were one of the few businesses who did not sack anyone during COVID and did not reduce anybody's pay during those times. We absorbed as much as we could and had to dig in deep from our personal pocket, but we thought it wasn't right for us to let go of anybody during COVID, because they would end up suffering. It hasn't been easy. There have been massive challenges from a financial and resources point of view, with people challenges and real mid-to-long-term consequences for our business. But I am confident that within the year we will have stabilised and recovered.

The journey has been interesting, to say the least – a massive learning because nobody has seen anything like COVID before and nobody has experienced this amount of lockdown in the past. We were already operating from the 'cloud' which made the implementation of working from home easier, but despite that, we couldn't roll out all our major communications projects as people couldn't go onsite. This also had an impact on how we managed staff, with retention becoming an issue, particularly in Perth where the mining industry is so attractive. But with borders opening, we are crossing that bridge and working through those challenges.

For us, it was a challenge of balancing the demands versus how to do things and make our clients' lives easier as we juggled with COVID. From the clients' viewpoint, we're still technology providers, so they expected us to do whatever it took to deliver what they're asking. We were trying to be as accommodative as possible. We had to rapidly adapt to the situation and this, I think, has been our biggest learning. We have developed adaptability across our businesses, from bulk ordering of hardware, to reducing supply chain risk and creating staffing flexibility. It's all about learning and looking back on how we have travelled together in those difficult times, it shows strength across the board from employees to clients. I think, in Australia particularly, we have managed it well. It certainly hasn't been a pleasant experience, juggling homeschooling as well on top of it all, but I have learnt a lot.

TELL US ABOUT DEALING WITH CONFUSION, CHANGE AND CONFLICT SINCE WE'VE BEEN IMPACTED BY COVID

Everyone has all been dealing with massive levels of stress. For business owners, we had to negotiate staff working from home. From a communications and IT perspective, there was a massive challenge for many, made more difficult because of implementation barriers. There was the challenge around the urgency of the issues of getting things in place, especially technology being a high-risk area for our clients. We were having to think bigger and more strategically during a time of crisis. There were concurrent challenges happening on multiple levels. It certainly pushed me to the limit in my capacity for decision-making.

It has been interesting too in terms of the increasing focus on issues like cybersecurity. IT issues suddenly became critical for businesses to understand. It has required leaders to change the way they value and priorities around these challenges. Being an IT company, cybersecurity is a core focus for us, and it started with us making sure our own business was secure; 'look at your own house, before you say anything about others'. We've had to ensure that we frequently visit our own technical environment, as this is key, hackers come up with absolutely brilliant ways of thinking and operating. We are constantly revisiting our system and meet with our technical group once a month to see what more can be done. We have set up multiple alerts in the system so we know immediately if anything happens.

We now work with our clients to help them understand this new operating environment. It's a different, technical and sometimes hard conversation, but I think with all the things happening in the current market, people are realising how important it is to look at the security side of things. Businesses are becoming much more aware and knowledgeable. There has been a change too in the types of cyber attacks we are dealing with, and I have learnt a lot around negotiation during high-risk conflicts.

When a client discovers they have been hacked, they panic. This is normal, but what we've found to be most important is that we don't panic. We must stay calm for the client, and if we are dealing with the hackers directly, we need to remain calm and focused. The moment you show any signs of panic, you're gone. I've learnt in negotiation that a lot of listening is required. Let me repeat – a lot of listening. A lot of hearing what they've got to say and responding 'based' on what they say. Negotiation is not something where you bring in *what you want to say* all the time. For me, it's about becoming seamless, in such a way that they should feel you're actually not making your own point, it sounds like you are saying what they're saying, but you still get to do what you want to do!

Negotiation happens in many ways in our day-to-day life, and I can't stress this enough, listening is key. Some people prepare what they want to say before they've heard the other side, and that will never work. If you want to achieve your outcome, you need to listen first. That's key in any negotiation. Losing your cool will not work. Intimidating the other person will never work, and raising your voice is a big no-no. What has worked for me over the past few years, as I have had to embark on complex, critical negotiations, is how important 'keeping your cool' is. Having a smile on your face, showing that you genuinely care for what other person is saying and bringing empathy is key to effective negotiations.

We all have had to learn to negotiate around complex issues at work and in our communities, but in anything and everything, listening and having your ears open all the time is absolute necessity.

TELL US ABOUT THE CRAICS, CROCODILE TEARS AND STANDOUT MOMENTS FROM THE LAST FEW YEARS

These stories highlight key moments for us over the past few years. I'm going to start with a sad story and then I'll finish with a happy note.

The first highlights the challenge of the new security environment. We were onboarding a new client, and they were in the process of transitioning from a different ID provided to us. During this process their server was hacked. They called us up saying, 'Something isn't' right.' It was at 10:25pm and I remember it so clearly. I had to pull in my team during the middle of the night; they had to come into our operations room so we could manage the crisis. Obviously, from the client perspective, they were panicking, and we shared some of that panic as well because we needed to look after them. We had to make time-critical decisions. How were we going to handle what was going to happen next, when minutes and seconds mattered and could result in the loss of all data? For everyone, it was like having a heart attack every microsecond. We were on our toes, trying to fix it, trying to bring it back and trying to protect everything once we'd brought the data back. We had to stay calm, focused and decisive.

The conflict was within our own group about how we were going to manage it. We didn't want to pay millions of dollars to anybody. We had to make sure that the client was with us at every step and there had to be deep trust. The CEO of the company came down and stayed with us throughout that night. The CFO was at home constantly in touch in terms of what was happening. Communication was on a knife's edge, balancing risk, because the second anything was to get out of control, we would need to communicate the relevant points to the relevant bodies, and that becomes a whole other intervention.

We contacted the hacker to see what they wanted and why. We wanted to initiate the negotiation process. We are lucky to have a great technical team which enabled us to back things up, and while they were doing the technical work, I was in constant negotiation with the hacker. My team were incredible, and together they were able to identify backups and restore the client's information. What really stood out for me was the conversation with the hacker, I had to keep them on the line long enough to allow my team to work their magic.

It was an incredible example of how my team pulled together during this crisis during COVID. It was extremely stressful and yet incredibly rewarding. We certainly couldn't have done it if we hadn't created trust within our team and with our clients. COVID has really made us hone our communication skills, both in moments of crisis and the everyday.

The other stand-out moment is related to our people. In Perth, things were going well, but because we couldn't travel there, we had to hire a manager for our service delivery. This role was highly paid, and we made clear that we expected the focus to be on aligning Perth and Melbourne into one group. With the best of intentions, it didn't work out. Employees started to leave because of the new employee's management style and their inability to manage people in a way that was consistent with our values. For me, it has been important to prioritise and care for my team. There is an understanding both ways, you have to be able to work together, and it is difficult to be a good manager unless you are willing to roll up your sleeves and do the work. In other industries it may be different, but in the tech space, this is very important. It soon became clear that there were differences of expectations and values. Because of COVID, I let it go on too long and didn't manage it proactively. I'm still managing the pain of that. It's painful losing clients and staff, but it's a more painful process because I didn't take action, and we let it go on for too long. It reminded me how important it is to clarify expectations and to have those hard conversations early.

Through all the painful moments, there have also been unforgettable stories. During COVID, one of our staff got her dream job. She came up to us to say thank you for all the support we had provided. When I hired her, she had no experience and few learned skills, but an amazing passion for PR. I watched her grow with us over many years, and to see her light up with joy for her new role is a beautiful journey for both for us. To see our people find their passion and see them fly! Running a business and making money is one thing, but it's about the relationships with staff who are relying on you, and many ways they're dependent on us. To look after our people holistically has been a key value for us in managing our business. And that's a lovely journey.

SHARE YOUR HACKS, INNOVATIONS OR LEARNINGS THAT HAVE EMERGED FROM THIS TIME

A key learning from this time has been how COVID has accelerated our adaptability, both as a business and within our team.

I have been delighted in how quickly we have been able to implement the things we have learnt along the way. We devised our own mechanism of implementing a certain technology in a very quick way. This has meant that if somebody wants some something done 'tomorrow morning', we can do it.

It's because we have invested in our people. We have made it okay to learn, to explore and reflect. I want to emphasise that in this technology space, you can't be static. You must reflect, test, learn and grow, otherwise you will be left behind.

Personally, I have learnt so much from the technical viewpoint. I have had to get my hands on the technical side of business, and that's been critical as a leader, as we have asked a lot of our team, and I needed to show them respect by being willing to get stuck in too.

LOOKING FORWARD, WHAT DO YOU THINK MIGHT BE SOME LASTING TRENDS OR INFLUENCES?

As leaders, we must be adaptable. We need to listen, to constantly learn and discover. We need to get used to being uncomfortable. This is important in the IT and communications space, but I'm not just talking about the technical aspects. I think that COVID has influenced the wider industry by showing that people matter.

It has been by nurturing and supporting my team that we, as a business, have been able to grow. It is the people skills, traditionally thought of as 'soft skills', that have best empowered me to deal with our biggest challenges, from supply issues to hackers. These are people problems, not IT problems.

For instance, learning the art of negotiation with your staff and not demanding your workforce returns to face to face won't work. Because if there are no staff, the job can't be done. And if there's no job and no clients, there is no future for your business. The question really comes down to, 'How are we going to work together?' The future trend, from the business leaders' point of view, will be about listening more to and working together with the staff. Gone are the days where you tell people what to do. That attitude is what needs to change and what, I think, is already changing. Then we need to embed that dynamic into our culture. Employees are always going to leave, but we can do lots to ensure that whilst they are with us, we work well together. There is a shift in the power dynamic – it is more mutual. We as leaders need to be more flexible in how, where and what we do together.

From a technology point of view, I hope that security is taken more seriously. What I see is that the one-man armies (solo business operators) and 'friend of friend' IT businesses are no longer able to keep up with the complex IT and security challenges we face. As businesses take their IT more seriously, we as an industry need to do the same to stay competitive. Our business has invested thousands of dollars to ensure we can provide the best service to our clients. It isn't simply a matter of set and go, we all need to be more proactive. We need to constantly check in on both our people and our technology!

YOUR TIPS FOR DEALING WITH PEOPLE DYNAMICS DURING CONFUSION, CHANGE AND CONFLICT

- Don't fight the change. Change is going to happen. Accept and adapt to anything that comes your way.
- Be calm when you're handling challenges. Go back to the old ways of writing down your challenges in business, with a pen and a notebook. And then do a flowchart on how to fix it.
- Don't assume anything. Get as clear as possible. I spend a lot of time making sure there is clarity, so we clearly see and then communicate the challenge. Never assume anything when you're talking to your team members. Make sure everything is 100% clear as some people don't understand what is being implied. Make it a more obvious source. So, be it client or staff, make things as clear to them as possible. Even if it takes longer to explain it, clarity is key.

BIO

Sree is director of business iICT Group with companies in Melbourne, Perth and presence in all states of Australia.

With extensive experience establishing business globally, she started her first company with her brother in her teens in India. When she migrated to Australia, she worked her way up to executive positions and undertook her masters in finance and financial management services. She now has multiple companies across Australia and wider and brings a focus on business leadership that drives revenue growth, she is also a customer excellence specialist.

As director for empower ICT, phase 42 and Business ICT Partners, her company is a leading provider of managed IT services, offering a holistic solution of services ranging from telecom, IT, cloud, IT security and more to simplify your business and telecommunication needs. With a passion for empowering her team to thrive, she has built a team of dedicated and skilled professionals. She also has an adventurous spirit and between being a CEO and mum, likes to explore the communities where her travels take her.

www.empowerict.com.au
linkedin.com/in/sree-swaminathan-b31859194/?originalSubdomain=au

SUSAN ANDREWS
ALLOWING THE FLOW

COVID challenged people's understanding of what constitutes violating self-determination and led to complex conflicts that continue in both public and private areas of our lives. It is that very fundamental freedom in self-determination that makes mediation so empowering and life so enlightening.

My eighty-five-pound lapdog, Segen, has provided me with many moments for laughter over the last few years. Segen has been a prominent presence during my remote online meetings, whether it be him greeting everyone virtually or serving as my sentry throughout my meetings.

TELL US ABOUT WHAT YOU DO AND WHAT YOU LOVE ABOUT WHAT YOU DO

I developed the service areas of mediation and negotiation with a focus on online dispute resolution (ODR) from what I consider a relatively unique experience and perspective, and I believe the COVID situation enhanced that uniqueness and its complexity.

In the transformative season of fall 2016, I had an epiphany.

It happened while I was being sworn in to the Kentucky Bar Association in the United States, with all the meaning and majesty of the state Supreme Court surrounding me, and while waiting to take the Kentucky Constitution's Oath of Officers and Attorneys, which included solemnly swearing that I had not fought a duel with deadly weapons. Although I found this slightly humorous, the purpose of this aspect of the oath is to drive home the point of not promoting vigilante justice, as Americanised Code Duello and de facto duels were historically an issue in Kentucky. Despite coming from the Wild West state of California, I couldn't help but be taken aback, though at the same time, in awe of the solemnity of such an oath. My pre-oath epiphany and consequent vision were that not only would I focus on developing a career in alternative dispute resolution (ADR), but that it would be solely in ODR.

I had numerous professional and personal reasons why this was my goal, and they have continued to be unwavering. Among them were that ODR made sense to me given the technological trajectory, and I wanted to operate from a remote and online location while having travel flexibility. I was already living a largely remote and online life between my urban homeland in California and what would eventually become my rural home in Kentucky. I imagined that people would likely benefit from such flexibility of being able to tend to disputes virtually from anywhere and at any time.

I have always been somewhat tech savvy and autodidactic, so trending toward innovation and technology has been natural to me. While I also remain someone who prefers the part of the world that is free from such things, and therefore, retains its natural beauty, I have always been cognisant of the need to address the detriments that can accompany technology, so that the benefits can be optimised. This unexpected development transformed my trajectory in ways I never imagined, especially when COVID changed our lives on so many levels and for such a long time, with the ripple effects ongoing.

Initially, I did not realise that ODR existed beyond the ecommerce context and that it had somewhat taken hold in the court context, but I knew that it had yet to truly take hold in the private context, as it was predominantly a scholarly subject in that area. But my perspective was clear and my research rapidly proved that it made sense for the private context in which I would be developing my practice. That was the lens through which I started to build my vision, harnessing available and aspirational resources with my creativity, collaboration, knowledge, wisdom and experience in business and legal contexts.

By summer of 2017, I was in Spain completing my formative mediation training in general civil mediation and attending that year's World Mediation Summit in Madrid. With a focus on international law during law school, among other interests, I already had internalised an internationalist perspective that informed my interest in domestic and international general civil, business and commercial dispute resolution. By summer of 2018, I was a volunteer mediator at the Fayette County District Court Small Claims Volunteer Mediation Program and had completed my formative negotiation training. By winter 2019, I completed my formative ODR training and was engaging in ongoing supplemental training on all fronts.

Little did I envision that such a catastrophic event as the COVID pandemic would be the catalyst which thrust the entire dispute resolution industry into the online environment. In fact, it temporarily closed areas that could not or would not go remote and online. This included in the private context, in which I was working day and night to develop my services, essentially from scratch, with a learning curve that I was successfully closing. And because ODR is clearly more than merely a Zoom meeting, these circumstances tested the limits of what people perceive as ODR and their level of comfort with such an environment for the negotiation and resolution of their disputes.

Before I had even completed integrating technology toward a seamless platform and streamlining my process, designing and launching my website, and beginning what I consider passively promoting my services, my vision, at least from the simplest remote online perspective, was no longer the exception but the rule, completely driven by COVID.

However, there was a complementary current awaiting me in the throes of this global pandemic tsunami, and I flowed with it. I trusted my instincts and intuition, which enabled me to continue developing my knowledge and skills, while both engaging me in leadership and speaking activities and continuing to work to bring my vision into the realm of reality. What I realised subconsciously, and in retrospect consciously, is that I was totally immersing myself both in the industry and in connecting with colleagues. This proved invaluable for productivity and peace of mind, at a time when I was not yet optimally postured for valuable business productivity, and while the personal circumstances of COVID, given the geographic distance from my family, were both difficult and devastating. This situation reaffirmed my focus and passion for remote and online communication for the purpose of dispute resolution.

Among my activities during this time, I was invited to serve as a member of the American Bar Association (ABA) ODR Task Force Working Group III. Our collective three years of work throughout the pandemic recently resulted in the publication of the *American Bar Association Section of Dispute Resolution Guidance for Online Dispute Resolution*. I served on the inaugural ABA Tech Expo (2020) Planning Committee and hosted two expo evening entertainment events – a virtual Kentucky bourbon distillery tour and tasting event with Woodford Reserve, and a virtual aerialist and actress interview and performance in Los Angeles, California, with Dreya Weber of *The Gymnast* and other films.

I became the first International Mediation Institute Qualified Mediator. I contributed to a law ebook and authored several articles for the legal website, Lawrina. I transitioned from Kentucky Bar Association Alternative Dispute Resolution Section treasurer to vice-chair and am now chair elect. And, I was appointed co-chair of the IMI ODR Task Force, among other leadership activities.

I was invited to, and participated in, speaking engagements for International Mediation Awareness Week (IMAW) 2022, ODR LatinoAmerica Expo Tech (2022), and Judicial School of the 4th Region Labour Court in Brazil International Seminar about the Juridical World's Challenges – Innovation, Collaboration and its Impacts in the Many Ways of Conflict Resolution, A Global Look at Mediation (2022).

I became a signatory to the World Mediators Alliance on

Climate Change (WoMACC) Mediators Green Pledge and then a member of its advisory board (2022). I completed William Ury's eXperimental Negotiation Initiative BB3 Workshop (2022) and am now a Possibilist, regularly attending Possibilist meet-ups. The BB3 Workshop is offered by William Ury and the eXperimental Negotiation Initiative (xNI). xNI is a program of One Earth Future, an incubator of innovative peacebuilding programs, and was launched in collaboration with Ury, co-founder of Harvard's Program on Negotiation, co-author of *Getting to Yes* and one of the world's leading experts on negotiation and mediation, to explore the obstacles to negotiated agreement and how to overcome them. xNI distilled Ury's nearly half a century of knowledge and experience with impossible conflicts around the world into a transformative mindset called Possibilism and a powerful method called BB3. We worked as teams to practice BB3 through interactive exercises, practical application, discussion and feedback. We learned how to apply the Art of Possible to transform conflicts and unlock progress. As a result, I participate in monthly Possibilists meet-ups with fellow Possibilists to share perspectives and gain practical ideas. I also became a certified dispute resolution analyst with NextLevel Mediation and expanded my services to include dispute resolution analysis, a service relevant to dispute resolution, decision-making and deal-making.

So, one can see how the ways I adapted to COVID have had a massive impact on my life. Now that the pandemic is more of a surf and less of a tsunami, I have returned to riding the wave of business development, while continuing to serve in some of the aforementioned roles, as well as new leadership and speaking or other engagements, including this publication.

I believe my decision to flow in the direction I did was largely due to the embracement I received from industry leaders with respect to my pre-pandemic development efforts, the breadth and depth of knowledge and skill I had developed during that time and possessed entering into the pandemic period. I am eternally grateful to my mentors and colleagues for their recognition and support of my efforts and evolution, which continue.

TELL US ABOUT DEALING WITH CONFUSION, CHANGE AND CONFLICT SINCE WE'VE BEEN IMPACTED BY COVID

Of course, there was much confusion and concern during the early months of COVID because life as we knew it and everything we thought of as 'normal', changed. And that change was increasingly intense. Every one of us was adapting to new ways of living our everyday life and adjusting to the toll it was taking in ways both similar and different to us all. Frankly, it was also shocking and surreal to so many if not most of us, and it put us on a path from which there was little, if any, likelihood of a return to what we think of as normal.

The most poignant professional point here is that the elements of mediation that I am so passionate about were alive and well within this magnificent community of professionals, as evidenced by our communication, cooperation and collaboration. Whether we relaxed and regrouped together over informal virtual happy hours from around the world or worked together in various formal capacities, we maintained these mediator qualities throughout. I believe this held me in good stead on both professional and personal fronts. And my strong and steady Doberman pinscher, Segen, was always by my side, true to his breed, along with my truly exceptional family and friends who certainly experienced this adventure with me, albeit from too far with respect to family and other loved ones. Nevertheless, we did our best and our best always passes the test of time. It is the significant universal loss of time due to reactions rather than responses to COVID that may not pass the test of time. Time will tell.

As to conflict, I am confident in and comforted by the fact that my dispute resolution background and concentrated interactions with colleagues possessing similar perspectives, mindsets and skills had a positive impact on my experience with conflict.

Specifically, people in general initially seemed to connect with little conflict, as we essentially accepted the challenges and changes COVID caused as inevitable, at least while we were developing an understanding of what we were dealing with. As time wore on, however, the effects of the various public and private reactions and responses to the threat COVID posed, exacerbated by the detriments of technology, increased concerns and conflict, highlighting the issue of self-determination. Self-determination is at the core of the dispute resolution process of mediation. Self-determination is also at the core of people's lives, if they do not violate other people's self-determination. COVID challenged people's understanding of what constitutes violating self-determination and led to complex conflicts that continue in both public and private areas of our lives. It is that very fundamental freedom in self-determination that makes mediation so empowering and life so enlightening. I believe that the issue of self-determination has emerged as the most compelling issue raised by COVID and meliorated by mediation concepts.

TELL US ABOUT THE CRAICS, CROCODILE TEARS AND STANDOUT MOMENTS FROM THE LAST FEW YEARS

How I have seen people respond to conflict challenges highlights how horses and other animals have been a special part of my life, and my natural horsemanship training and experience have, in part, inspired my approach to communication through relationship awareness, engagement, self-awareness, authenticity, creativity, flexibility and leadership. Reflecting on my relationship with my Doberman, Segen, and with horses, reminds me of the authenticity, grace and dignity with which animals engage the world, and how I strive to communicate efficiently, effectively and ethically with others based on this sensibility of communication. This has become increasingly important due to the way in which the impacts of COVID and simultaneous challenges have made such communication much more difficult.

My eighty-five-pound lapdog, Segen, has provided me with many moments for laughter over the last few years. Segen has been a prominent presence during my remote online meetings, whether it be him greeting everyone virtually or serving as my sentry throughout my meetings.

Of course, with heightened emotions, we are often provided with times when we could laugh or cry, and where possible I choose laughter. These occur mostly for me when I am living in the present moment, in which I remember that I and my family, Segen and other loved ones, are alive and well enough to have a reasonable quality of life, if not more, and that we have the blessing of technology, despite all its detriments, to bridge the difficult distance divide so that we can see and hear each other synchronously. Without the ability to be with my family in this way, it would seem even more impossible and incomprehensible. This is an example of optimising the benefits of technology.

During my work, I have observed how people sometimes respond to conflict challenges with more of a reaction than a response, thereby increasing conflict and making it more challenging to decrease, if not resolve, conflict. This is among the reasons why I developed expertise in dispute resolution analysis, became a certified dispute resolution analyst, and offer this as one of my services. I value the ability to acknowledge people's subjective aspects of conflict while guiding them through a process that enables them to focus on the objective aspects of conflict, so they can efficiently and effectively identify and prioritise the interests or objectives underlying their positions, and then identify and prioritise alternatives for addressing and resolving such conflicts, all from a more logical than emotional perspective and position. I believe this leads to more lasting, and therefore, more successful outcomes.

The great is the willingness to embrace this type of sound and successful approach to resolving conflict, the bad is the unwillingness to at least respond rather than react to conflict, and the ugly is to refuse to operate in good faith, and to refuse to, at least, do one's best.

SHARE YOUR HACKS, INNOVATIONS OR LEARNINGS THAT HAVE EMERGED FROM THIS TIME

A learning I have taken from this time is the relative peace and productivity that can come from the adage of *not doing anything when you don't know what to do*, allowing time and space for ideas and answers to emerge, if they will. This speaks to the flow I experienced when adapting to how COVID impacted me professionally.

Because I was among the relatively early practitioners to train for and develop remote online services, the demand for my research and insights eclipsed everything else, as people sought me out as a thought leader or authority in this area. My natural leadership skills and business vision were valued by dispute resolution professionals, and this further enhanced my appreciation of the industry, due to the cooperation and collaboration I experienced with colleagues.

In summer of 2022, I realised the opportunity to finally spend always invaluable time with my family for the first time since the inception of COVID. Accompanied by Segen, I drove the several thousand miles each way cross-country to and from California, navigating a new landscape through a new lens, both of which sustained that sense of shock and surrealism, with stress, sadness, excitement, strength, and above all, gratitude.

I also had the opportunity to reflect on all that had transpired. This reflection reinforced to me how critically important it is to operate from a position of strength, not weakness. This is where the distinction between responding and reacting, the ability to both embrace emotions and empower logic, moving beyond one's subjectivity to a level of objectivity that enables self-awareness rather than self-absorption, exercising some common sense and compassion, and successful decision-making all become so important to realising relative peace of mind and productivity, if not also positivity.

By not doing too much more than following my instincts, intuition and the energy that was generated, I was able to harness positive momentum, however imperfect, and experience the relative peace and productivity that flows from that. I use the term 'relative' because it is a qualifier to this state, being less than what we might ideally aspire to, at least from the perspective of someone who tends to be a perfectionist! For me, it necessitates having some humility, faith (however one defines that for and in oneself), flexibility, hope, curiosity, joy, gratitude and perseverance. Nevertheless, I believe it can hold one in good stead, because these things tend to generate strength.

BIO

Susan Andrews is founder and principal of Andrews Dispute Resolution and an attorney, mediator, negotiator and dispute resolution analyst. She is also chair elect of the Kentucky Bar Association Alternative Dispute Resolution Section, co-chair of the International Mediation Institute (IMI) Online Dispute Resolution Task Force, and a member of the American Bar Association (ABA) Section of Dispute Resolution ODR Task Force, which is comprised of experts from around the world who worked for the past three years to produce the recently published *American Bar Association Section of Dispute Resolution Guidance for Online Dispute Resolution*.

With many years of business and legal experience in general business and Fortune 500 multinational companies in a wide range of industries and sectors and in corporate legal departments and law firms in a wide range of practice areas, Susan's expertise in online dispute resolution (ODR) is focused on the online negotiation, mediation and dispute resolution analysis of domestic and international business and other general civil disputes as well as facilitating decision-making and deal-making.

What Susan loves about what she does is her use of empowering neutrality to guide parties in dispute, conflict, decisions and deals, so that they can achieve a peaceful and successful resolution. She especially loves the self-determination aspect of the service areas in which she practices, optimising the parties' control over their outcomes in these processes.

andrewsdisputeresolution.com

VIKRAM SINGH
BRINGING PEOPLE UNDER THE TREE

It's the process not the word that matters, we have to connect people with a process they are familiar with.

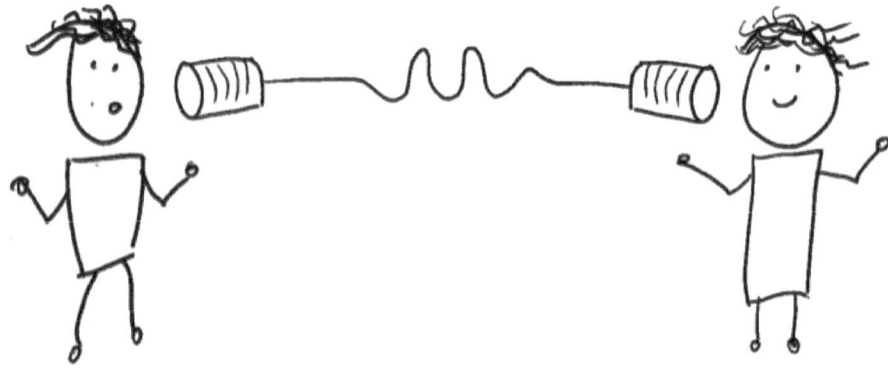

I have really learnt the power for allowing the conversation to flow. I don't have time to focus on a script and what I need to say next, and this is what I keep saying about mediation. You don't have time to think about, *Oh, what is that person? What is that person all about?*

TELL US ABOUT WHAT YOU DO AND WHAT YOU LOVE ABOUT WHAT YOU DO

I'm a lawyer who is a full-time mediator and peacemaker and a part-time golfer. I'm promoting mediators and mediation around the world, and I must be doing something right having been invited by Sarah to contribute to this book. I live on computer and mobile screens around the world and on the golf course. I get to connect with wonderful people around the world and to have lovely conversations; that's what I love about what I do. My wife and daughter keep asking me: *why do you spend so much time promoting mediation? Why don't you do your work instead?* We have to live with the *new normal* but the *always normal* is that doing work is gauged by money in the bank. They are not wrong as we have to eat, play golf (some lucky ones), travel and spend time with family – and the world is one family. You may ask, why my wife hasn't divorced me? I'll tell you – I don't know.

My advice to people has always been to resolve disputes in an amicable manner, although my entry into the legal profession was through litigation at the Supreme Court and High Courts in India. I totally relate to Mahatma Gandhi's experience when he said: *'My joy was boundless. I had learnt the true practice of law. I had learnt to find out the better side of human nature and enter men's hearts. I realised that the true function of a lawyer was to unite parties riven asunder. The lesson was so indelibly burnt into me that a large part of my time during the twenty years of my practice as a lawyer was occupied in bringing about private compromises of hundreds of cases. I lost nothing thereby, not even money, certainly not my soul.'* This has been my philosophy as a lawyer. The legal profession is known as a noble profession, and I love practising for this reason.

From the time I started my own practice, my focus was on prevention and pre-emption of disputes and to nip them in the bud. This required creating a space to bring people together at all levels in organisations, to have conversations and to create an atmosphere of collaboration. Mediating without using the word mediation. People around the world may not be familiar with the word *mediation,* but they are familiar with the process. We need to connect them to the process and to those with the mediator mindset.

Even while handling an adversarial process, I've reached out to the other side, because that's the kind of person I am. When your intentions are good, people trust you and you can assist them in resolving their disputes.

TELL US A LITTLE ABOUT HOW COVID IMPACTED WHAT YOU DO AND HOW YOU ADAPTED

Just before COVID hit, I had already decided I was going to practice as a full-time mediator. Promotion of mediators and mediation wasn't on the agenda at that point in time. COVID had a very positive impact on my life. With COVID came lots of time to play golf (my golf course was closed only for a month), connect with people from around the world on social media and attend lots of webinars on various aspects of mediation. This gave me a broad idea of what's happening in the mediation world. It also brought out issues which were common around the world. My way of adapting to the change was to be the change. I took it upon myself to promote mediators and mediation. I wanted to question the box of mediation which was going around the world. I wanted to dig a little deeper. I call this the dispute resolution revolution.

On one side, we were talking about mediation as being the best thing that can happen in terms of dispute resolution, and on the ground, it wasn't really happening. People who have the mediator mindset and are passionate about mediation and want to be full-time mediators are not being able to do that. What is missing? To answer this, I started having conversations on various topics and then more conversations, and today (as I write this) there are 483 videos on my channel. That's 483 lovely, insightful and thought-provoking conversations with wonderful people from around the world. I've organised various shows and events:

Evolution of a Mediator
The focus around the world is on 'training'. That's become an industry. There are people with the mediator mindset who have the skill and you don't need to 'train' them. Institutions were claiming to 'make' mediators and people were being misled that training, accreditation and certification would open a career path. You don't make mediators or become mediators in 'forty-hour factories'. It's also demeaning and disrespectful to mediators. Whenever I use the word 'mediator' it refers to someone with the mediator mindset. The only people who 'make' mediators are the people in dispute. They can 'make' anyone they want, a mediator. There's lots that goes into having a mediator mindset. Upbringing, value system, life experiences and lots more for which we may not even have words. To highlight this, I started a show called *Evolution of a Mediator*. It started with the journey of Ken Cloke, who doesn't need an introduction; Ken has provided the foreword for this book.

In Conversation With a Beautiful Mind
Lots of people couldn't put a face to a mediator although they

may have heard about mediation. With development and urbanisation and lots more factors which I won't get into here, people with the mediator mindset in communities and families lost their value and respect. I started a show called *In Conversation With a Beautiful Mind* where I have conversations with people with the mediator mindset. Let people put a face to mediators. Let them know that mediators are wonderful and special people.

Mediation In Our Culture & Traditions
People around the world may not be familiar with the word mediation but they are familiar with the process as it has been used for time immemorial. A collaborative approach to dispute resolution has been used by families and communities including indigenous and business communities for centuries and has passed on from generation to generation. We have to go back to our roots and move away from an adversarial approach to dispute resolution to a collaborative approach. To highlight this, I organised an international symposium of *Mediation In Our Culture & Traditions* in August and September 2021. There were ninety-seven speakers from forty-five countries. Sarah was one of them. Amazing speakers. Wonderful, interesting and insightful sessions.

Heart Soul Spirituality & Mediation
Heart, soul and spirituality play an important role in relation to the mediator, the participants (not parties) and the process. To discuss this, I organised an international symposium on *Heart Soul Spirituality & Mediation* in April 2022. Lots of interesting thoughts and perspectives. Sarah was a speaker, and an interesting thought that came out from her session was *Mediators as Leaders & Leaders as Mediators* which is one of objectives of the

work I'm doing for the promotion of mediators and mediation.

World Mediators' Conference

Ken Cloke is the face of my *Dispute Resolution Revolution*. If people want to put a face to a mediator then it's Ken's face they should see. I'm celebrating his birthday, 18 May, as World Mediators' Day. I organised the *World Mediators' Conference* which began on 18 May with Ken celebrating his birthday with us. The Conference went on until 30 June with ninety-three sessions on various topics. There were eighty panelists from around the world. Hopefully, in 2023 we'll have even more participation.

Indigenous Peoples & Mediation

To take the discussion further on culture and traditions, I organised an international symposium on *Indigenous Peoples & Mediation* in August 2022. We have to go back to our roots and move away from an adversarial approach to dispute resolution to a collaborative approach.

Colonisation, Decolonisation & Mediation

Colonisation has had major impact on dispute resolution and the impact has continued in decolonisation. To discuss this and the colonisation of mediation which is taking place, a class distinction is being created between people who are qualified, accredited and certified as mediators by organisations and institutions and those who aren't (savages?). There are mediators in every corner of the world who are trusted by people and they neither have, nor need, any qualification, accreditation or certification for the wonderful work they are doing in families and communities. To discuss these issues, I organised an international symposium on *Colonisation, Decolonisation & Mediation* in September 2022.

Philosophy & Mediation
I organised an international symposium on *Philosophy & Mediation* in November 2022. An interesting takeaway was that mediators are philosophers in practice and mediation is philosophy in practice.

Neutrality & Mediation
Neutrality has been very commonly associated with mediators. To question and discuss this, I organised an international symposium on *Neutrality & Mediation* in December 2022.

Forum Series
In my *Forum Series*, I've had discussions on:
- *Mahatma Gandhi & Mediation*
- *Socrates & Mediation*
- *Women & Mediation*
- *Ombuds as Mediators & Mediators as Ombuds*

Talking Books (Because some of us don't read them.)

Mediator Reflects with Michael Lang
Michael is known for his work on reflective practice and has reflective practice groups around the world. Michael had members of his Irish practice group on the show and it was the first time that discussions of a group were being recorded, while going out live on YouTube.

Mediator Experiences
This series was to have mediators talk about their interesting experiences not necessarily in a mediation. It began with Weinstein JAMS International Fellows talking about their experience

with the fellowship. The last episode was with Alexandra who is from Paris and is at the Poland-Ukraine border, working with refugees.

TELL US ABOUT DEALING WITH CONFUSION, CHANGE AND CONFLICT SINCE WE'VE BEEN IMPACTED BY COVID

My experience has been that people want to have conversations. This is true for people around the world. Conversations which don't have an agenda. Conversations that are informal and unstructured; they just flow organically.

People need a safe space to have those conversations. I'm really selective of the people I bring into the space. Humble people who have humility. No supremacists of any kind, be it colour, nationality, race, language, wealth, qualifications and more. No patronising.

People from around the world want to connect and understand each other, collaborate with each other. People want to move away from activism, advocacy and politics. That's the platform I've created. A space where people can be their authentic self.

When you speak from the heart, listen to the heart and connect to the soul, those connections happen instantly even in the online world. Most of the people who have participated in my events, I've met or even spoken to for the first time when they've come into the Zoom meeting. The connection has been instant, and we've had long, wonderful conversations. We have connected on a deeply spiritual and human level.

TELL US ABOUT THE CRAICS, CROCODILE TEARS AND STANDOUT MOMENTS FROM THE LAST FEW YEARS

The funniest story that comes to mind is about a conversation with someone in a country where there is a lot of tension and conflict at the moment. We were on a WhatsApp video call. During the conversation the person was telling me how he has to use a virtual private network (VPN) and how he believes the government hacks computer systems. In the middle of the conversation, the call was disconnected. I was trying to get back in touch with them and it wasn't connecting. I was sending messages but they weren't going out. With WhatsApp you can see by the 'ticks' when your message has been sent, and then if it has been read by the receiver. I wasn't getting any ticks for my messages which means that the messages weren't even being sent. I sent a message to my wife and the same thing, no ticks. Who was the person I was speaking to? Should I have done a background check? Even wondering if the government had done this! Racing thoughts, to the moon and back in a split second. My wife sent a message to her sister – same thing, no ticks. Panic sets in. My wife called her sister to tell her that my WhatsApp had been hacked. Her sister tells her that she also cannot send messages.

A feeling of self-importance sets in. Everything I touch will turn to gold, everyone I connect to on WhatsApp will be hacked. We made calls asking people to not send us a message on WhatsApp. I thought either the government had hacked my system or blocked my access because they definitely don't have better things to do!

Then, my wife discovered in a news report that there was a major outage with WhatsApp across the world. What a laugh we had, made us cry.

There are lots of heartwarming stories. Elena, who lives in Siberia, sent a lovely New Year's message in a video that she made standing outside in the cold. It was such a warm message, so touching. It's messages like this that makes connecting with people from around the world such a special and fulfilling experience.

SHARE YOUR HACKS, INNOVATIONS OR LEARNINGS THAT HAVE EMERGED FROM THIS TIME

The biggest learning, is that we need to hack the colonial mindset towards disute resolution that disputes are resolved in courts and lawyers have to be a part of it. The connection of courts and *free mediation* is the worst thing that has happened for mediation around the world. The judiciary is the most inefficient institution in almost all countries if not all. For their self-interest, they are promoting mediation, although mediation and courts have nothing to do with each other. They are totally different methods of dispute resolution. The courts are taking it to an extreme with mandatory mediation, the foundation of which is so weak and has led to and will lead to absurdities such as imposing costs when the court decides that the mediation wasn't done 'in good faith', or that the rejection of an offer was unreasonable.

Mediation in the court system in the United States for the last fifty years hasn't helped develop mediation as the first port of call. It hasn't led to people practicing as full-time mediators, apart from very few exceptions. It's just led to lawyers controlling the process and using mediators. People come into the system to be recognised by lawyers for private work, which they don't get, because lawyers want to use the free services *volunteered* by mediators. Mediators get disillusioned and move out from the system, and in most cases, out of mediation. A new lot comes in and the cycle continues.

This has to stop. Courts have to stay away from mediation. Mediators have to stop giving their services for free. People should choose mediation because they want to collaborate.

We have to question if it's mediation at all or just 'settlement meetings'. The most inefficient institution forces you to go for a process where you are told that it's better for you to settle to save time and the costs involved in going through the inefficient institution. Is this party self-determination. You don't choose the process, you don't choose your mediator, you don't choose the settlement for the right reasons.

The colonial mindset continues when it comes to mediation legislation.

The other learning, is that even a multi-million-dollar dispute can be resolved through mediation conducted totally online with participants in various cities and countries. No paper. No travel. It's given me so much time to promote mediators and mediation and play golf. Good for the environment. Good for the participants. Great for the mediator. It can't get better than this. Win-win-win!

The most important learning is that you can create connections online. Deep and meaningful connections.

LOOKING FORWARD, WHAT DO YOU THINK MIGHT BE SOME LASTING TRENDS OR INFLUENCES?

The structure of society has changed over time. From communities to individualism. There could be lots of reasons for that which is best left to sociologists to study. People with a mediator mindset will have a very important role to play. They will need to be the ones to bring communities together. When there is a community atmosphere, it is then that a collaborative and amicable dispute resolution process will be appreciated and utilised. When there is a sense of belonging, the resolution will take into account the larger interest of the community. This applies to local and global communities.

Towards this end, I'm creating a World Mediation Circle – a World Wide Web of mediation. This will help people in resolving their disputes in an amicable and collaborative manner and attempt to heal and strengthen relationships. I'm creating mediation circles to bring moral values (not value), principles and an ethics based humanistic approach to dispute resolution where heart, soul and spirituality play an important role. Mediation circles will be created in communities around the world. Communities could be:

- Place-based
- Identity-based
- Issue-based
- Business
- Organisational

The mediation circle will have mediators, peacemakers and people who want to resolve disputes in an amicable and collaborative manner (participants). It's important to distinguish between peacemakers and mediators. Peacemakers have the skill to bring people together and mediators have the skill to assist them in resolving their disputes. Both these skills are important. The people with the mediator and peacemaker mindset will be identified by the communities themselves. Mediators and peacemakers are all out there in communities. In families. In schools. Power and money are valued today. We have to create an atmosphere where mediators and peacemakers are valued.

We are all a part of a global community; therefore, we have to think global and act local. This even applies to dispute resolution. To illustrate, the Global Climate Change Mediation Circle will be a web of climate change mediation circles which will be created in every community, right down to a village. Conversations in relation to climate change don't just need to happen in some global forum. They need to happen in every community, to have a local and global impact. We have to get everyone along if we want a meaningful resolution.

The World Indigenous Peoples Mediation Circle will be a web of mediation circles with a mediation circle in every indigenous community around the world.

There will be a web of mediation circles in every community, every school, in every country. These will not just resolve disputes at the local level but will also create an atmosphere for conversations on national issues.

We have to *bring people under the tree*. It's the importance of moving away from the mediation room and the mediation table. Moving them under the tree brings an informality to it all. We have to allow people the room to connect where they are. Mediators need to get out into the community to bridge the gaps. This is a move away from the clinical box of mediation that is being distributed around the world. This is recognising that people in dispute are more than a transaction. This is about a humanistic approach to mediation.

We have to move people away from divisive politics, the seed of which was planted by the divide-and-rule policy of the colonisers. It's about building trust and a deep level of connection first, before we start talking about the dispute resolution process. And again, my mantra: 'Process is important not the word – we need to connect them with process *they are familiar with* if it is to have meaning.'

The long-term objective is to have mediators as leaders and leaders as mediators.

This is part of my mediation vision 2026 for the evolution of mediators and mediation.

YOUR TIPS FOR DEALING WITH PEOPLE DYNAMICS DURING CONFUSION, CHANGE AND CONFLICT

- The human touch. Beyond all the difference that may be created between people, there is something that connects us at a deeper level. We have to connect to that core. Everyone is a good human being until proven otherwise. Innocent until proven guilty. The human-to-human connection can be positive and can also have a negative effect as COVID has shown us. It depends on what you are transmitting.

  When we connect to the core, when we connect with the heart and connect to the soul, we discover that there are no differences between us.
- Just do it. Making a difference doesn't have to be complicated be it in sports or otherwise. I'm promoting mediators and mediation from a small table with an old laptop, an internet connection and me (my authentic self). That's all that's required. If you really want to do something from within and you don't want anything out of it, then you have everything you need to start. You just need to take that first step. That first conversation. That first video.
- Creating a safe space. When Andrea, who's based in Ireland, tells me that I've created a safe space for people around the world, it feels really nice but it also comes with a sense of responsibility. I'm very selective of the people I bring into my space. No negative energy. No supremacists of any kind be it

colour, nationality, race, language, wealth, qualifications and more. As Michael Lang puts it, it's my living room.
- Enjoy the edutainment! Be a part of the dispute resolution revolution! Join the World Mediation Circle.

BIO

My name is Vikram Singh but I'm better known as Mediator Vikram. I'm an advocate who is focused on practicing as a mediator which is very rare in the world and I'm trying to change that by promoting mediators and mediation around the world. I'm based in New Delhi, India, but live on the golf course and on computer and mobile screens around the world. I'm a full-time peacemaker and a part-time golfer.

My focus has always been on eliminating unnecessary legal expenses for clients as also the need for litigation. My expertise has always been in taking pre-emptive and preventive action to prevent and avoid disputes and if they do arise then resolving them through non-adversarial methods of dispute resolution which are not an alternative but Appropriate Dispute Resolution (ADR) methods for Amicable Dispute Resolution (my ADR). My mission is to promote mediation and spread its awareness so that mediation becomes the primary method for resolving disputes. People in some parts of the world may not have access to Justice or may be denied justice because 'justice delayed is justice denied' but we can give them access to mediation, not just at their doorstep but inside their home through online mediation. As internet accessibility and connectivity spreads all over the world, we should eventually reach even the remotest village. We have to develop a culture of mediation and a culture of peace with collaborative effort within communities around the world. This has to be done at the grassroots and should start in schools for children to imbibe it themselves and influence the community. As Mahatma Gandhi said, 'If we are going to bring about peace in the world, we have to begin with the children.'

mediatorvikram.com
linkedin.com/in/mediatorvikram/?originalSubdomain=in
youtube.com/c/MediatorVikram
linkedin.com/in/MediatorVikram
facebook.com/MediatorVikram
twitter.com/MediatorVikram
instagram.com/MediatorVikram

TRENT PETHERICK
ASSESSING COST DIFFERENTLY

When we are dealing with dispute and people in conflict, you have to be able to get behind the technical side of things and get to the heart of what the problem is. Mostly it's people problems.

So often I see people suffering from depression, unable to sleep over the anxiety of litigation.

TELL US ABOUT WHAT YOU DO AND WHAT YOU LOVE ABOUT WHAT YOU DO

I was a partner at a leading provincial law firm in New Zealand before heading to Western Australia in 2011 to join one of Perth's largest law firms as a senior associate. In 2012 I established Petherick Cottrell Lawyers in Mandurah. It was a means to bringing specialist employment-related litigation assistance to residents of Mandurah and the surrounding area.

I enjoy resolving conflict problems for clients. It can be challenging, nevertheless, if you're organised in your approach and you plan strategically, the results follow. I love this work because of the diversity it provides. You never have the same problem twice. For the first two years of my career, I trudged the usual path for the top academic graduates. I worked in a large commercial law firm completing highly technical and complex amalgamations, corporate restructuring and insolvencies. It was so tedious that I was ready to quit at the thought of this being my daily life for the next fifty years. Fortunately, I was able to follow my attraction to the litigation aspect of law. It's more time-consuming work but I find it very satisfying and rewarding. I am constantly dealing with people from a variety of diverse backgrounds and find it deeply satisfying to be able to aid them in resolving their legal problems.

Over the years, I've gained much insight into people and how they work. Different personalities deal with disputes in several different ways. There are those who come in wanting to fight as a matter of principle; they don't care what the cost is. Then they get to mediation and the reality kicks in. Whatever the dispute, we really want to help people to move on. To achieve this, clients need to know their prospects of success in court – along with all the costs of litigating to the bitter end; that is why this conversation is so important. From my heart, I have never encouraged litigation. We don't need the additional work and our clients don't need the stress. It's wonderful that, over the years, the acceptance of mediation has grown, and the courts are becoming more onboard with it.

TELL US A LITTLE ABOUT HOW COVID IMPACTED WHAT YOU DO AND HOW YOU ADAPTED

COVID was frustrating because everything came to a halt. As lawyers, we tend to be busy. Many of us actually want to resolve things for our clients so they can move on. COVID meant that everyone stopped for a while. Courts weren't operating fully, we weren't able to see people face to face and there was so much uncertainty. Here in Western Australia, we have been lucky compared to so many other states and countries, but we were also still trying to find our way forward.

It has been a mixed bag for us. There was no slowing down of work and then a rapid rise in further work. We were rushed off our feet. Like many, we have been navigating staffing challenges too.

We have focused on helping our clients get good, practical outcomes and perhaps, because of that, we have been able to expand. We have upgraded our building and created some hugely exciting collaborations. Perhaps COVID has encouraged that. It has helped us connect with other experts to help fill the gaps. We have found alignments outside of the legal community, with like-minded passionate professionals, including a partnership with an excellent HR firm. We are looking at flexible ways to service our clients in ways that are expertise driven. This includes our

HR Legal Connect membership initiative that offers unlimited legal support. We work alongside the HR team with a focus of effective advice and strategy from the outset to stay out of court altogether. We stay in our lane, and we mutually benefit. It is exciting, and we are seeing real benefits both in terms of working closely with clients to avoid claims and the growth of our firm.

What we have seen in conflict response to this time is an understanding that mediation is often the right fit. When we want something resolved, we talk to the right people, and we adopt mediator skills. In a criminal case, we might go down with the file to the prosecutor's office and then just sit down and sort it out. We've done that on many occasions. We've resolved many things with simple face-to-face meetings. I believe as a profession we need to be promoting the culture for mediation. There are so many benefits and I'm seeing 80-90% of problems resolved in mediation. How has COVID influenced this? I think it has brought the dispute resolution professionals together – courts, lawyers, mediators, judges and the parties – who all just want to focus on getting on with things.

For those in business, it seems there's been a shift that had to happen around the way everyone talks about dispute resolution, instead of going straight to court. Yes, you still need your lawyer, but you don't have to have a protracted and expensive 'fight' to get a good outcome. You're better to focus on outcomes at the start and be pragmatic. That might mean throwing say $5,000 at the problem – we politely call 'f@@k-off money' – because the claim lacks merit but it's usually better to end the dispute than litigate further. Some parties go into the fight out of principle that is usually understandable given the emotion involved, but it's almost always better to be pragmatic. It is our job to help clients overcome the emotional response and look at the advantages of conflict resolution. It's smart to mediate matters early and get back to business quicker, so you can get on with making money in your business or get on with your life generally and focus on those things, not on litigation.

TELL US ABOUT DEALING WITH CONFUSION, CHANGE AND CONFLICT SINCE WE'VE BEEN IMPACTED BY COVID

I think everyone's a lot more emotional. COVID has put stress on everyone and that has flowed into the workplace. There seems to be increasing anxiety in workplaces and with our clients. I'm not sure if it is COVID or a combination of factors, but people don't seem to put things in perspective as much as they used to. They don't seem to be as resilient, and it's unfortunate. I think that this actually makes mediation an even more important process. Going to court is a really tough process and we don't often talk about the emotional cost; it adds heat to the conflict and the stress. So often I see people suffering from depression, unable to sleep over the anxiety of litigation. It could be the smallest things, you know, just neighbourhood disputes or things that get out of perspective. And people really do stress a lot. I get frustrated with lawyers being overly technical at the wrong moment because mediation is not about showing how smart you are. When we are dealing with dispute and people in conflict, you have to be able to get behind the technical side of things and get to the heart of what the problem is. Mostly it's people problems. It's not about the law, it's about how you can resolve the conflict.

I guess my belief is that people are naturally emotional, but we believe we're completely logical. When we buy a car, we want the shiny 'red' car. We might have convinced ourselves logically that our red car must be safer, but often this is just an emotional decision. That's where we justify the rationale.

We put a logical framework over our disputes because we like to think we're logical. But so often, the conflicts and disputes we deal with as lawyers are more often a question about emotional issues. For instance, where people have been dismissed. The dispute is as much about the fact the employee feels hurt. They may have worked for an employer for fifteen years and then they are abruptly and without warning made redundant … 'And they didn't even follow the process!' It is understandable they feel this is unfair. We spend so much time at work, often more time than we have with our families, so it can feel extremely hurtful.

TELL US ABOUT THE CRAICS, CROCODILE TEARS AND STANDOUT MOMENTS FROM THE LAST FEW YEARS

I wanted to share a story about mediation and how powerful it can be. This story is about a 'very financial' church. It was one of those high-energy churches. Many members left money to the church and the church became wealthy over a number of generations. On a particular occasion, the youth group kids decided to surprise the pastor one Friday night. They pulled the curtain back to the young pastor's office, only to reveal him having sex with someone else's wife. Its hard to say if the kids, someone else's wife or the pastor got the biggest surprise. Well, you can imagine, after the illicit ministering of the pastor was found out, things very quickly started to fall apart! This was a very complex dispute. The board wasn't effective, and people were very emotional. The church was facing closure from the Attorney-General, not because of the pastor's activities, but because of the highly dysfunctional board. Closure could mean redistribution of all church funds to another charity. It was decided that mediation would be the way to go, and we engaged a top person in New Zealand. We knew that if this wasn't resolved, there would be no good outcomes for anyone. This mediator was incredible. He was very sharp and allowed everyone to be heard with a clear focus forward. He asked questions like, 'What are the best outcomes for you and everyone, short of compromise?' We ended up getting a resolution. It was a hell of a job, and even though there were a lot of people 'hating on this person', it's all about compromising and looking at your best alternative.

There are a lot of disputes that are never going to be resolved in the court process. Rarely can a client go to court and be completely vindicated. The process is expensive and exhausting. Mediation often presents a healthier alternative. It's realising 'look, this is stressing everybody out, so let's look forwards and see what we can all get out of this'. We often use mediation when we have friends who go into business at the expense of their relationship. Things can turn very nasty. Staff and clients then begin to leave. The business starts going downhill fast. You can go through the courts and absolutely destroy everything, or you can get to mediation and say, 'Right, let's bang some heads and work out how we can resolve this.' And if you're sitting in your office sending letters to the lawyer on the other side, they write snarky letters back. It's a game of tennis with legal letters. We both know we're not getting anywhere; we're just entrenching our position. The other side gets angrier and angrier because they miss something in the lead up that was critical. You've just got to get around the table. The sooner the better.

SHARE YOUR HACKS, INNOVATIONS OR LEARNINGS THAT HAVE EMERGED FROM THIS TIME

My first standout lesson is the power of being heard and the power of an apology. One of the things I have seen work well in New Zealand is the power of the apology (interestingly not done so much in Western Australia). In NZ I have seen plenty of examples where the employer is honest and says, 'I'm had to sack you – I'm going broke,' and the other person often responds with, 'Honestly, I just wanted an apology and an acknowledgement that you didn't treat me fairly,' and then they make restitution with something as simple as, 'I know you go cray fishing every week, and I actually want to resolve this matter, so perhaps I can get a dozen crayfish and some beers,' and suddenly they have made their own deal their way! What enabled this outcome is that everyone said what they needed to, they talked and there was an acknowledgement and an apology. Even if the excuse was, 'I was going through divorce, I was downscaling my firm, and I probably didn't handle it properly.' When we understand how powerful a genuine apology is, it allows everyone to better work through all these conflicts.

If we want sustainable solutions to our conflicts, we must work through it. We must be respectful and appreciate that culture is important to the process. We often just need to be heard. It might sound simple, but listening is laying the groundwork for understanding the way the parties feel.

My second stand-out lesson is the importance of assessing the cost. It's important that we start expanding the way we assess conflict risks and costs. As lawyers and parties, asking questions like, 'What are the risks if we keep going down this angle from a litigation perspective?' It isn't just the litigation costs, it is the emotional cost, the financial costs, the loss of opportunity costs. These risks need to be factored in the equation. Rarely are these costs good, even if you do win. We all know how stress negatively impacts our health, our relationships and the quality of our life generally.

This means being pragmatic is vital. I was once acting for a young woman involved in a sexual harassment case where she alleged sexual harassment by her employer. During this mediation, the other party decided to bring his wife. One imagines it was for moral support, but it certainly illuminated his ignorance of the severity of his actions. When my client started explaining about 'how it made her feel to have a sleazy old boss', I was watching the wife carefully and I literally saw the light-bulb moment. Her face read 'I could see you doing it that way' of her husband. He became very uncomfortable when the wife wanted to meet in private with the mediator. I knew at this point it was just a matter of details. Whilst this is lighthearted many years later, it is also a good reminder of how we assess cost, how we fixate and entrench our thinking, and the power of listening to make wise decisions.

We are also seeing more companies assessing costs in terms of their reputation. It's becoming increasingly important that they don't want it known that they've got a loose-cannon manager or unsafe work environment in other ways. It's not a good look for the mining sector, for example, when they're trying to recruit to more women, if they've got a sexual harassment case ongoing. That is why mediation can be so beneficial because of the confidentiality of the process and the speed of resolution.

LOOKING FORWARD, WHAT DO YOU THINK MIGHT BE SOME LASTING TRENDS OR INFLUENCES?

I think there'll be increased recognition of mediation and the importance of the process. Ideally, if I had my way, people would be engaging in mediation much earlier. I understand, it has been 'how we do things', but the court process creates fear and is often just traumatic for the parties. There's all this posturing and entrenching of positions before you even get in front of the judge. This is usually when the courts send you for mediation; a sort of the last-ditch effort before your list for trial. You go through these interlocutory steps, which cost a lot of money and don't really achieve much at all. It's frustrating, because we are focusing on everything but the substance of the dispute and getting it sorted, dragging it out before we can get to mediation.

There needs to be more education to create greater awareness. I get frustrated by my own profession, because I don't believe they think 'outside the square' nearly enough. They just do what we've been doing for a hundred years. They wait for the court to tell us to go to mediation. I mean, if you're getting paid a high hourly rate, surely you can think outside the square? I use victim offender mediation quite a lot in criminal cases. I used to be guilty of thinking it was the 'soft option'. Then I attended one. There were tears all around. The young guy that we were acting for broke down and cried when he heard and understood how his actions had affected the victim. It was immensely powerful for all parties. Importantly, the victims. Allowing the offender to see and fully experience the harm they have caused must reduce recidivism.

As a lawyer, I'd also like to see more experienced mediators that are passionate about it. Mediators who roll their sleeves up and get stuck in. Their capacity to resolve things should be renumerated accordingly. We need to value how important this skill is.

I see some mediators who seem to almost lack commitment to the process. They are often a bit stand-offish and seem to lack energy. They like to hear from the lawyers because it keeps things moving quickly. My belief is that it's important that we allow space for the clients. They must have the opportunity to speak and be heard, and to release their emotions. This is vital so that we dive deeper than the technical conversation. In my experience, most parties want to line up the employer and say, 'This is how I felt when I had to go home and tell my spouse that I didn't have a job. My kids were in tears. You know it really hurt, and I think for you to just send me a text to say I'm dismissed, that stinks.' The mediators that allow for that to happen, generally in my experience, get the best results.

What I would love to see is mediators with more nuance who are able and willing to get into the emotions, to the humanity of a dispute within the resolution process. But the mediator's job is also to help the parties move past the emotional and focus on the rational. There's a meeting in-between the two areas and a skilled mediator can hold this space professionally. It is extremely difficult to be a skilled mediator and the choice of mediator is accordingly tremendously important to the outcome.

YOUR TIPS FOR DEALING WITH PEOPLE DYNAMICS DURING CONFUSION, CHANGE AND CONFLICT

Get independent advice. It might sound self-serving, but when you are in conflict, you get caught up in the emotion of it and then you just get entrenched. The conflict festers and then it becomes personal and that's never good.

I know for sure that if employees got independent advice early when the problem starts at work, not when the disciplinary process occurs, outcomes will be much better – emotionally, psychologically and financially. The same is true for employers. Get objective advice and keep things in perspective, instead of leaving it to end up in an unfair dismissal that will be challenged because that's when things get nasty and affect people's lives greatly. When you're in conflict, it's not just the legal advice you should be basing your decisions on. It's a whole pile of information that helps you make good decisions.

Stay focused on resolution. Ask yourself, *What is your end goal?* because you don't want to get caught up for a year bickering, likely dealing with a worker's compensation claim and psychological abuse allegations. It's often better for your life, for your marriage, in your relationship with your children and people that are close to you, to resolve the matter. I see so many people are just a mess because of what's happened. And you know, litigation can drag on for years, and whilst we don't talk about it, often the people involved end up having psychological problems. To achieve an effective outcome at mediation it is essential to be well advised on the law and effectively represented. The process falls down without this.

Keep your cool. If you find yourself in conflict, don't aggravate the situation. It can be tempting to lash out and react to the situation, but keeping your cool is going to save a lot of problems down the track. How it is dealt with will set the tone of resolution. That might mean staying quiet, it might mean walking away. You're not giving up; you are choosing to stay cool which is a smart move in any conflict. Of course, collect the evidence over time but remain calm and in control while you do it.

BIO

Trent Petherick has almost thirty years' experience as a senior litigation lawyer and was partner at a leading firm in New Zealand before moving to Western Australia in 2011 and commencing at one of Perth's top-tier firms as a senior associate. In 2012 Petherick Cottrell Lawyers was established and was a means to bring specialist legal assistance to the residents of Mandurah and surrounds.

Trent's experience sees him provide excellent results for his clients in the areas of employment and criminal litigation. Trent's tenacious and dynamic approach ensures that the interests of the client are met without unnecessary cost and time, and he has quickly developed a reputation within the region as an effective litigator. This includes successfully defending serious criminal matters on a regular basis in both the District and Supreme Courts. Trent also completed a Masters of Law at the University of Melbourne in employment law, graduating in 2014 with Honours.

petherickcottrell.com.au

SARAH BLAKE
CONCLUSION
PULLING IT TOGETHER

The opportunity to gather such a diverse and talented group of people has been a great privilege. In the dispute resolution world, we often work alone, gathering only occasionally either at conferences or for Zoom presentations. The same is often true for those business leaders who joined us. Being busy has become our norm and we forgot how valuable those moments of connection are. To be able to dive down into 'real' conversations about the things that matter to us has resonated with an inner yearning.

Sometimes conflict just overwhelms; it becomes like an avalanche that becomes bigger and bigger, you lose control and the consequences can be huge.

What was interesting about interviewing our authors and reading their contributions was a consistent acknowledgement of the mental cost over the past few years. For them, for their clients and in what they are seeing in their work, there is no doubt that we have all been under sustained pressure, dealing with grief and constantly having to adjust and change. This has resulted in a deep creep of exhaustion and decision-making fatigue. It isn't surprising then that all those frustrations, personality clashes and differences are resulting in more conflicts, micro-conflicts and division. People's tolerance, patience and hope has been tested and we all need to reset.

I have seen a huge increase in the conflict work that comes my way, but I have also seen a shift in the types of conflicts that are hitting the media across industries. From the sporting world, politics and business, differences of values, of expectations and a realigning or prioritisations have brought to the surface conflicts which are complex, multidimensional and have generally been simmering quietly for some time. There seems to be two types of responses emerging: 1) the people who are leaning into the change, who are adapting and seeing this time as an opportunity and 2) the people who are bedding down and becoming more positional, looking back on the 'good old' days. But before you judge these people, as most of them are just doing the best they can, remember, there has been confusion and high rates of change across the board. For many of these people they are seeking something to hang onto and control. Control creates an illusion of safety. Added to this is the preference to blame the other. Brené Brown (Brown, 2015) talks about blame and how it is much easier to blame than to take responsibility. It is easier, as it then requires less of us. Ultimately, these conflicts and challenges we are seeing aren't generally caused by COVID but rather

the fact that we ourselves have changed. It is impacting how we deal with those points of frustrations, confusion and difference.
- Those passive-aggressive comments are no longer acceptable.
- Those poor working conditions are no longer tolerable.
- The performance of an individual carried by others cannot continue.
- Profit at the cost of the environment is not okay.
- Fuelling division, either for political or personal, no longer holds our attention.

In my work as a conflict strategist, my job is to elevate leadership decision-making when there is confusion, conflict or change. It requires us to assess the conflict holistically, to really understand what the conflict is about and to help leaders find clarity about what they want the future to look like. It isn't just about helping people reach a resolution, it's about helping people gain clarity, make decisions and act in ways that align into the future. And as we navigate beyond COVID, these skills will become increasingly important. It requires us to acknowledge the complex, beautiful and messy humanity of us all. This means understanding that our emotions, our needs and our hopes matter and shape what we do and how we make decisions. For leaders and mediators, the questions is less 'how do we get people to the table?' and more 'how do we help them shift to future focus?'

For our leadership, the past few years have been testing. It has pushed decision-making to its limits and required a capacity to connect and empathise with your people. As mediators, we practice in the business of 'bringing people together'. What we perhaps are rediscovering is that the ritual allows us to connect to a deeper level, and for those leaders able to create those rituals of connection virtually, they have boosted those connection points. But this book has highlighted consistently some themes that I think will continue to influence us all, moving forward, in how we deal with our people and how we make decisions about the BIG issues facing us.

OUR PEOPLE – OURSELVES

COVID has made us confront our mortality. Too many people have been lost, families divided and priorities have changed. For workplaces, be it in corporate or community spaces, the realities of this 'new future' are being navigated on the go. But what our contributors have all shared is an observation that power dynamics have shifted, and managing teams, people and difference requires something more of leadership.

There is a listening, a renegotiation of expectations that is occurring. As Jo McMullan talked about; it is going back to basics and creating a culture that is change resilient. But don't mistake this as a 'soft process', a giving in to demands – it's not. What this book also shows me is that leadership will require us to be focused, confident and strong. For many of the mediators in this book, there is an acknowledgement that there is a hard, realistic edge to us, but there's empathy in that hard edge too. Perhaps what we are seeing is a recognition of the need for balance – that peaceful place in-between. Certainly, our ancient traditions understood that wise decision-making comes from a place of calm and of peace. So, as we gravitate into the future, perhaps we should be looking to balance emotions and logic, balance our people's needs with business; a recognition of the importance of nuance and that not everything can be 'fixed' or made perfect. Let me say that again: stop looking for perfect. Even when you fail, it's not the end of the world. Failure is rarely as bad as you think it will be, and if you can shift your mindset there's opportunity that comes from it. So as leaders, as problem-solvers and as people in conflict, there is power in recognising that some differences are just that, and leaning forward is simply managing those tensions.

But it isn't just a change in how we engage with others. This time has also impacted us as individuals. For many, this has been a time to reassess priorities; how you spend your time and where. Burnout or mental exhaustion is real, and this constant pressure isn't sustainable. So as we look to collaborate more effectively, and across industries, we also need to make time for our own wellbeing. Paul Sills said this eloquently when he said he has learnt to be 'kinder' to himself. As we balance all these new opportunities, we also need to balance the joy, the happiness and peace in ourselves.

OUR ENVIRONMENT – OUR VALUE

One of the overwhelming shifts that our authors have all identified to have emerged since COVID is the prioritising of environmental issues, of sustainability. There is an increased awareness of how we, as humans, are impacting the world and a willingness to take responsibility for this. These shifts have included the commercial valuing of wind and solar energy, an upsurge in investment by companies in sustainable practices and communities vocalising their commitment in politics, boards and at the local level. This is an exciting and optimistic shift but it also comes with layers of complexity in conflict around this space. Looking forward, it seems the questions will be, 'How do we work these challenges out?' and, 'How do we do this in a way that gives voice to the least powerful, not just the most vocal?'

This has implications for dispute resolvers and business

leaders alike, as they all seek to discover what 'good governance and good process' look like. These are the negations that are ripe for division and 'high conflict' as people become embedded in their own sense of 'right' and 'truth'.

Perhaps, the conflicts in the past were more lineal, as Mikel Sanz Peña discusses, they focused on money, profit and growth, thereby making contracts much easier to resolve. What we are seeing now, however, is a heightened prioritisation of values-based issues. We now need to consider politics, science, reputations, relationship, non-human entities; it's all the messy stuff! The situations are complex which necessarily requires a multidisciplinary response. It is not enough to be experts in 'maritime law', we also need process experts and people who can manage people. What this means for resolving these complex issues is that we cannot do it alone!

Perhaps, what we have gained over the last few years is an increased understanding, but as we evolve into the future, it's action that is now required. It isn't enough to know the issues, we now need to do, to heal and to create. This is us taking our future to the next level.

Reading the chapters and speaking with the authors in this book has been a humbling experience. It has reminded me that there is so much to learn from each other. We've had to adapt quickly, often with little reflection, and if we don't pause, take those moments to reflect on what worked well and what didn't, we miss opportunities for learning. That is the risk when you shift from crisis back into 'business as usual' without taking the time to debrief, to reflect. Perhaps, if there is a key tool that COVID reminded us, it's that it's important to pause. To reflect and not react. To pause our egos, to allow ourselves a moment of vulnerability to say, *How am I?*

My hope is that this book challenges you as leaders to reflect on your own discipline of dealing with conflict. Do you react or respond? Do you listen or jump into a fight? Are you okay with the discomfort, or do you seek to avoid it? I want to encourage people to listen to those nagging feelings of discomfort, the unpeaceful feelings, because these too are sources of information. It's you saying, 'We've got work to do here, there's something to be done.' This mindset shift allows us a moment to transition from the negative of the conflict into opportunity. In recognising both the craics and crocodile tears that exist in this complex space, we are reminded about perspective, about choice. Yes, these things can be painful but often there are moments of joy, laugher and light. This is the pace of desolation and innovation.

For leaders, we know that we are the ones who set the tone for problem-solving and resolution. As we transition out of the crisis of COVID, now is the time to reset expectations about how we deal with the problems that impact us. And I hope that these chapters fill you with ideas and inspirations, with practical hacks that you can take forward. As conflict increases and competition heats up, now is the time for us all to rise up and speak out for a different way of dealing with conflict. Together we can shape a future where conflict becomes a vehicle for constructive change, innovation and peace. This conversation starts with each of us taking responsibility for how we deal with the complex people dynamics around us. Choosing to future focus with curiosity, strength and grace.

With peace in our hearts.
Inspiration in our minds.
Courage in our actions.

BIO

'Building a world where leaders see conflict and opportunity for innovation and change.'

Award-winning conflict strategist and mediator, TEDx speaker and bestselling author, Sarah Blake, elevates leaders, empowering them to overcome conflict barriers. Bringing clarity to complex decision-making during confusion, conflict and crisis, she helps transform problems into opportunities.

As a second-generation mediator with over twenty-six years of experience, Sarah has engaged in some of the most complex problem situations across remote Australia and into the Pacific. She has worked within corporate, university and NFP sectors delivering intervention and is increasingly sought by leaders struggling with the impact of conflict and change.

Working across industries has provided opportunities to engage with bodies such as the World Bank, BHP, Australian Federal Police, Land Councils and national, state and local government. Sarah has delivered talks across the world, both in person and online, and is considered a thought leader within the industry. This has enabled her to contribute to international advisory boards and support the development of the next generation of peacemakers.

She is an accredited mediator with Resolution Institute and International Mediation Institute and is the Australian Ambassador for Mediate Guru and an Ambassador for Think Network UK. Sarah is also a multiple-bestselling author and regular contributor to media in Australia including television, radio and print where she is talking all things conflict from growth leaderships, people dynamics and culture.

smblake.com

www.ingramcontent.com/pod-product-compliance
Lightning Source LLC
Chambersburg PA
CBHW020316010526
44107CB00054B/1865